HIDING IN PLAIN SIGHT

PREQUEL TO - FROGS SNAILS AND MOBSTER TALES:
GROWING UP IN AL CAPONE'S SHADOW

ROBERT J TEITELBAUM

CAROL A TEITELBAUM

TEITELBAUM PUBLISHING COMPANY

Hiding in Plain Sight

ROBERT J. TEITELBAUM

CAROL A. TEITELBAUM

Prequel to:

Frogs Snails and Mobster Tales: Growing up in Al Capone's Shadow

TEITELBAUM PUBLISHING COMPANY

Copyright © 2017

Robert J. Teitelbaum

Carol A. Teitelbaum

All rights reserved.

ISBN: 978-0-9993519-3-2

www.frogsandsnailsandMobstertales.com

❀ Created with Vellum

PROLOGUE

By the time I started school at four years old, all my classmates knew we had Mob connections.

It wasn't easy growing up in a home dominated by deceit, forced upon us by the company our mother and father chose to keep.

My parents were Mob lawyers, deeply involved in the activities of the Chicago, New York, and California branches of organized crime.

I found myself in difficult situations because my parents, Abe and Esther Teitelbaum, had told my siblings and me to never tell anyone anything about our family, and especially about their clients.

As the saying goes, "You are only as sick as your deepest secrets."

My parents did not know that my older siblings told those secrets to their school friends.

Many of the parents would not let their children play with us. To remedy this, our parents started spreading money around to the PTA and political races. They allowed the community to have parties at our home, the Loveless Ranch, and to swim in our Olympic-size pool.

After a while, our home life changed. Our parents were often away. My brother, three sisters, and I were left in the charge of Pop's California bodyguard and Loveless Ranch manager.

For now, I want to share stories that both my mother and father shared with my wife and me.

I fact-checked them through the Freedom of Information Act, finding some to be factual, while others mostly true. There is no way I know of to verify them.

Here are some things I know with absolute certainty: My father grew up in New York. His childhood friend was Benjamin Siegel. (He was often called "Bugsy" by people who were not friends, and always behind his back. My father never called him that nor let anyone around him do so.)

His friends included Meyer Lansky and Salvatore "Lucky"

Luciano. I know that he was a lawyer who represented Alphonse Capone, his brother, Ralph, and the entire Capone family.

His clients included fourteen top members of the Chicago Outfit. He had dealings with Joseph Anthony Tony "Big Tuna" Accardo, who was also known as "Joey Batters."

In California, he represented the likes of Mickey Cohen, Jimmy "The Weasel" Fratianno, and the hit man, Frank Bompensiero.

My great-uncle, Harry Teitelbaum, was associated with Murder, Inc. in New York.

Quite a litany of friends and clients! Some, like Al and Ralph Capone and Ben Siegel, were mostly characters in the stories Mom and Pops told. I was too young to interact with them. I was just a kid running around.

What shaped my parents' lives also shaped mine. Because I grew up around the Mob, I was influenced by mobsters. While the mobsters weren't exactly good role models, I learned a great deal from them.

I learned to keep my mouth shut when I had nothing to offer, especially if someone in charge was speaking. I learned to honor my father and mother, but not in the ways you might expect. I learned the art of evasiveness (when necessary), and of telling the truth to the people who counted.

I learned to take care of myself when I was in a situation that required muscle, but to project a quiet calm so as to fall under the radar when in public.

I learned that revenge could be taken only when everyone has your back.

Not only were my parents associated with organized crime, but two of my mother's uncles, Leopold Benjamin Melnick and his brother, Felix, were arsonists associated with the Chicago Mob in the early part of the 20th century.

Uncle Ben inexplicably went on to become a lawyer whose clients included the cream of the Chicago Mob, including Al Capone.

(How my parents got to be Capone's lawyers is a grand story with at least nine versions, depending on which of my mother's siblings is telling it.)

Uncle Felix went on to become one of the founders of the Movie Projectionists Union, a nationwide union that was "mobbed-up," as they say.

The toxic environment that infused my youth continued into my adulthood.

When I got out of the Marines in 1965, my father was convicted of land fraud.

Although there were many crimes my father did commit and was never charged with, this conviction was strictly political.

He had a client with 1800 lots in Moro Bay and sold them through Prudential Bank.

Abe was in Chicago when a check for the broker arrived in the mail at his home in Beverly Hills. This check was to be given to the broker for fees. Instead, the check was cashed and "endorsed" with his forged signature.

Finally, the government had something to pin on him.

In 1972, Abe was given a questionable sentence. In prison, after suffering a heart attack, he was assigned the job of supervising the menu at the kosher kitchen and of tending the loquat trees. He worked out daily and lost weight.

He became the jailhouse attorney for some of the most dangerous inmates. Abe got them released by reviewing their files, finding the precedents that helped to re-open their cases. He drew up writs (handwritten!) that succeeded in court to release six of his "friends" from prison.

He now had the reputation of being the legal mind at Elm Hall, Chino Prison!

In 1948, Abe left my mother for a twenty-something woman he met through two of my aunts. They had brought her to my parents' home for a holiday party.

While observing the beautiful home and family, she decided she wanted what Esther had. She went after it and she got it: Abe, a big house, lots of money, and children. (She already had one daughter. She and Abe would have four more children together.)

In later years, Abe's connection to his first family became spotty. Money became an issue because he was not sending us anything. My mother had stopped practicing law after my baby sister passed away in 1948. Despite my mother's knowledge and skill, she was breaking down and could not stay the course. She was unable to take care of her children or her wandering husband, who would show up when it was convenient for him.

We went from being filthy rich, being driven to school in limousines (with bodyguards for protection), hosting parties for the New York Mob, Chicago Outfit, California politicians, and local charities, to becoming paupers, in what seemed to be a rapid fall from grace.

All this contributed to my character development during those formative years.

I could have gone "down the rabbit hole" and followed in the footsteps of the people I admired. But, I didn't. I married young, had kids, and found a sense of responsibility, for which I credit my wife, Carol.

I was waist-deep in that rabbit hole when Carol pulled me out. It is, in fact, due to her insistence that we are writing this book together.

By making stories public, I no longer get to keep them secretly bottled up. By telling these tales, I cleanse myself of attachment to them as being mine, alone. I am free of them because I give them freely to you. Still, they are mine to retell without changing the facts to suit my audience.

I think you'll have much fun unwrapping this gift. At times you'll laugh. You may even cry. But, I promise you'll have a grand time as you gain insight into the infiltration of organized crime into my family, and into American society.

This story began long before I was born. It ends with the ink on these pages.

1

BEGINNINGS

My story has three beginnings.

The first was when immigrants on both sides of my family arrived in New York and Chicago. The second was when my parents were born into an already bustling trade of crime. Finally, my story begins when I could first observe how things worked around our house.

When my grandmother, Tillie, got off the boat at Ellis Island, she arrived with her brothers, Felix and Leopold, who, because "Leopold" sounded too Polish, became "Ben."

In 1903, Ben and Felix, along with Tillie and her husband, Herman, settled in Chicago's North Side.

The area was one of those places where immigrants, especially Jewish, Italian, and Irish, settled.

All three groups were considered by "polite" Chicago society to be untrustworthy, lazy, dirty, and downright disgusting--immigrant scum coming to take work away from "real" Americans.

Signs proclaiming no Irish allowed, or no Jews, or even no Italians, were common at the turn of the century. Work was hard to find. Many of these immigrant men turned to the only steady work they could find: a life of crime.

In many cases Jews and Italians worked together. They had a great deal in common: they were smart, industrious, ambitious, and focused on success.

An alliance seemed to be in the stars.

They banded together against the Irish, who both groups saw as crude, good for muscle, but never for thinking or planning. With crime being one of the few available avenues for work (violent sports like boxing was another), the twenty-ish Ben and Felix found their niche.

They became part of a gang of firebugs working for James "Big" Jim Colosimo, then the boss of organized crime in Chicago. Jim emigrated from Sicily to Chicago when he was only 17 and started his career as a petty criminal. He captured the attention of a few notables. They made him a precinct captain and, later, their bagman to collect and distribute dishonest money to pay bribes. (This gave Colosimo the political connections that helped him rise to power as a Mob boss.)

While family stories among ten siblings vary, I gathered that Ben and Felix were the two hoodlums in charge of this gang.

What is certain is that in 1914 the pair was tried and convicted of arson-for-profit, an insurance fraud scam. Along with other members of this gang, the Melnick brothers made the local papers as "well-known firebugs" and appeared in court. Funny thing, though--neither spent a moment in prison. As far as I can tell, their trial records have disappeared.

There are no records of the conviction with the Cook County Clerk's Office, nor with the Illinois Prison Board of their incarceration.

The only hints of this conviction were found in an old newspaper clipping and in a not-so-well-researched book about mobsters in the early 20th century that has long since disappeared from publication.

Traces of the article can still be found on the Internet. I don't put much value on the prejudiced tone of the work.

Ben became a lawyer representing hoodlums and thugs in Chicago, a pretty tough go for a convicted felon. Felix was shipped off to New York, where the brothers had connections, including my great-uncle, Harry Teitelbaum.

Not only were there tough Jews on my mother's side who began their careers in organized crime soon after they got off the boat, the same is true of my father's side, even before he was born.

2

ESTHER MELNICK

Esther Melnick was feeling irritated on the morning of Yom Kippur in 1923. She was preparing the breaking-of-the-fast dinner for her parents, grandparents, two uncles, and nine siblings, and doing this all on her own. Her older sister, Rose, was absent from the preparation duties. No one could eat until sundown.

Her mama, who was never taught to cook as a child, was impressed by the fragrant smells flowing through the house.

Checking the simmering soup or stopping to help a younger sister with her homework or boyfriend troubles were daily distractions in Esther's life.

Esther, the third child of this large family, along with her older sister, Rose, had been in charge of parenting their younger siblings for as long as they could remember.

Esther, nineteen years old, had excelled in school and studied hard to maintain an A+ average. She dreamed of earning a law degree, which would require breaking into the "boys club."

Setting the soupspoon aside, a solemn Esther pulled from her apron pocket an application form to John Marshall School of Law. She smiled. She had filled it out days ago and it was due this day before 5:00 p.m. As she refolded the form to return it to her pocket, her mama came running into the kitchen.

"Your sister Rose has run off with a young engraver who works at the San Francisco Mint. They're getting married! She's moving with him to the West Coast!"

Mama's face was red and she was sweating, obviously upset. "You must give up your silly dreams about going to law school! Instead, you will take charge of my six younger children, do the cooking, cleaning and keeping order in the household. Esther, you must do this for me! I am needed to work with your papa at our venetian blind store, but, Esther, there's a silver lining--you'll get Rosie's big bedroom!"

Esther put her hand on her mama's arm.

"No Mama, I will never give up my dreams."

Taking off her apron and handing it to her mother, she walked out of the kitchen, upstairs to her bedroom. She dressed, grabbed her school records, and walked out the front door.

This was the first time she had ever defied her mother and she felt great! Looking down Clark Street, she took a deep breath and walked to the bus stop. Riding on the bus with the money for law school in her purse, Esther watched the streets go by until she arrived at the entrance of John Marshall Law School. She smoothed her skirt and bravely entered the building.

The office was empty except for an elderly woman who seemed to be in charge. Esther introduced herself. "Good morning, I'm Esther Melnick. I'm here to enroll." She handed the woman the folded form.

"Good morning to you, Miss Melnick. I'm Professor Riley and I'm waiting for Dean Lee. We are meeting to go for some coffee."

Professor Riley seemed to know the procedure and handed Esther more paperwork to fill out.

"Do you have school transcripts?"

Esther produced the transcripts, took a seat at the desk, and proceeded to fill out the forms.

"Esther, your grades are stellar. You must have worked very hard."

"Yes, it took a lot of work to get these grades."

Esther had been told the cost of law school was one dollar per week. While filling out the forms, Esther realized that she didn't have enough money. She had $40.00 in her purse, the money that she'd saved during four years of high school. The cost of law school was now four dollars per week.

Dean Lee entered the office and greeted by Professor Riley.

"Dean Lee, may I introduce you to Miss Esther Melnick? She wants to go to law school."

Dean Lee sized up this woman. She was only five foot three, but there was a strength about her that he had rarely seen. He was curious to find out who she was.

Esther was on the brink of tears. "I'm so sorry, but cannot afford the four dollars per week."

Professor Riley, handing over Esther's school records, said, "Dean Lee, may I suggest that you see these transcripts before letting Miss Melnick go?"

"It is my pleasure to meet you. Please sit down and let's talk. Esther, did you study Latin?"

"Yes, for two years."

"Tell me, please, the meaning of *dubia meliorme interpretari debent?*" Esther answered without hesitation.

"Doubtful things should be interpreted in the best way."

"*Corpus delicti*, the meaning please?"

"The meaning simply asks, where is the body? A person cannot be convicted of a crime unless it can be proven that the crime was even committed."

"Tell me why you want to go to law school?"

"You can see by my transcripts that I am a serious student. I love research and finding answers to difficult questions. I always wanted to help people while being independent and self-sufficient. Attorneys are respected and it doesn't seem that there are many women in this field, present company excepted, Professor Riley. I simply want to prove myself."

Dean Lee smiled. "Esther, what is the definition of *mercennariis tuis?*"

"You're hired? Oh, yes, I'm hired!"

"Esther, sometimes money is not paramount. Today, opportunity is knocking on your door. My last law clerk just graduated and I am prepared to give you a job as my assistant. The pay is six dollars per week. If you agree, you have a job."

"I accept, and thank you very much!"

"Esther, now you can afford your education. You will be working in the administration office doing my research and typing my correspondence. You may study for your exams in my law library. Esther Melnick, welcome to law school! I will see you Monday morning at 9:00 a.m."

Esther, overwhelmed by her good fortune, thanked Dean Lee and Professor Riley, letting them know that she must be home before sundown. Esther had her future in her pocket and she rushed out to catch the bus.

She walked up the street just as the sun was going down and arrived in time for the breaking of the fast meal with all her family, except Rose.

After dinner, Papa and Mama sat down in the living room to talk to Esther. Mama began but was shushed by Papa. "Esther, we are proud that you have taken care of our home while going to school and getting the grades we wish the rest of our children would get. We know how hard you are working at your studies while helping to raise your younger siblings. Mama and I have talked to Sarah and she will take over watching the children. Things will be in good hands."

With a broad smile and twinkling eyes, Papa continued. "You have our support to go to law school. We have some money put away and we wish that you would accept our offer to help you."

"Mama and Papa, I am so relieved! I have a job with the dean of the law school as his law clerk. I would like to stay at home until finishing."

Papa and Mama agreed and they hugged, which rarely happened.

3

MISGIVINGS

Mama was giving unwanted advice, as usual. "Esther, I want you to talk to Uncle Ben. He's an attorney with clients that pay real money. You can work with him when you finish law school."

"Mama, Uncle Ben is a criminal attorney defending some very despicable people. I did not decide to become a lawyer to engage is such sordid affairs."

Mama, always with a quick response, countered, "Esther, they pay well. Notice how smartly Ben dresses, and he has a real leather valise and alligator shoes."

"Okay, Mama, I'll talk to Uncle Ben," Esther retorted, just to end the discussion. She had no intention of actually talking to Uncle Ben.

"Mama," she quizzed sarcastically, "Is it true that Uncle Felix and Ben were arrested in 1914 for being fire starters, working for Big Jim Colosimo's South Side Gang? When Big Jim was murdered, didn't Ben go to law school to work for Big Jim's nephew Johnny Torrio, the head of the South Side gang called the Chicago Outfit?"

Mama wrinkled her brow and made a guttural noise that Esther had never heard before.

"Esther, they were only small fires, really tiny, your uncles never went to prison for anything."

Esther knew most of the stories about Uncle Ben and Uncle Felix, who came to America in 1903 on the ship, "Philadelphia." After moving in with their Chicago family from the Jewish Pale of Settlement in Poland, they became troublemakers, causing the family grief, but spending little time in jail. They never seemed to get caught with their hands too far into the cookie jar. They were lucky to have been allowed into America.

Ben and Felix settled in Chicago and immediately made contact with some bad apples, including Big Jim Colosimo's South Side Gang. Ben was attending accounting school, and Felix was working as a projectionist at the nickelodeon by day. At night they were working as arsonists for the gangs.

Esther, researching their files, found out that the pair was arrested in 1914 and sentenced to twenty years in prison for arson-for-profit. It's amazing that they never spent one day in prison! Someone paid someone off and records disappeared.

Felix was sent to New York City to start the new, corrupt projectionists' union. Ben was sent back to school to become an attorney, to represent Big Jim Colosimo.

Ben became friends with Big Jim's cousin, Johnny Torrio, when Johnny came to Chicago to be second in command of the South Side Gang. Johnny Torrio, another Brooklyn, New York boy, now known as "The Fox," helped build the Chicago Outfit. His talents as an organizational genius were widely respected by the major gang bosses in the New York City area. He was considered the biggest gangster in America.

After Prohibition went into effect, Torrio immediately understood the immense profits bootlegging could bring and urged Big Jim to enter the business. Big Jim refused, fearing that the expansion into other rackets would draw more attention from the cops and and rival gangs.

Torrio was angered and things got worse when Big Jim divorced his aunt.

Torrio learned from Uncle Ben, who was now one of the South Side Gang's attorneys and his friend, that Big Jim was going to have Johnny whacked for being too ambitious.

On May 11, 1921, Johnny sent Big Jim to his restaurant to

meet with bootleggers. When they didn't arrive, Colosimo left in anger. On his way out the door, an assassin leapt from the cloakroom and gunned him down. No one was ever convicted of that crime, although Frankie Yale and Al Capone were always suspects. After Big Jim was murdered, Torrio took over The Gang.

Over the next few years, with Al Capone's help, Torrio turned the Outfit into a criminal machine. During the Prohibition years, he kept his connections with the Chicago Outfit, which proved profitable for everyone involved.

Bootlegging brought in $100 million a year at the height of Prohibition. The Outfit controlled most of the liquor trade on the South Side. An Irish-American gang led by Dean O'Banion dominated the North Side. The two sides had bitter fights for control of the city.

In 1924, O'Banion sold a brewery to Johnny just before the police raided it. Torrio was arrested and received a nine-month prison sentence. He vowed revenge. On November 10th, O'Banion was murdered by gunmen in his flower shop.

Esther weighed all sides as to whether or not she wanted to get involved with Uncle Ben. Right now, however, she had to finish school and work for the dean. After all, she had made a commitment to him, and to concentrate on her studies. Her plate was quite full.

She pacified her mother by telling her that she was waiting for the right moment to talk to Uncle Ben. That seemed to be enough to satisfy Mama.

4

TILLIE & THERESA

Attorney Ben Melnick introduced his sister, Tillie Melnick, to Alphonse's mother, Theresa Capone.

They became fast friends. Two immigrant women with similar interests made for a perfect and long-lasting friendship.

A beautiful spring day found Tillie and Theresa, a pleasant Italian woman, sitting at the kitchen table of Theresa's home. They were enjoying a plate of noodle kugel, a tasty Jewish dish with egg noodles, raisins, and a rich sauce of cottage cheese or ricotta.

"Tillie, what is this wonderful sweet pasta you brought? This is so good, my boys will love this, *mi piace*."

Tillie smiled, knowing she was making an impression on

Theresa. "Next week at my home, we will make noodle kugel together."

Theresa, not wanting to be outdone, smiled back. "Tillie, I will come to visit and bring tomatoes and garlic from my garden. I have seven children and I'm always cooking. I can teach you how to make my sauce for pasta."

"I have ten children," Tillie bragged, "and my daughters do most of the cooking. I'm so glad my brother introduced us. We have a lot to talk about."

"My sons, Alphonse and Ralph, are your brother's clients. Both are in the same business, sort of. Let's not talk about this for now."

"Did you know, Theresa, that we eat off two sets of dishes? One set is for meat and one is for dairy. It has been our dietary law for the last five thousand years."

"Tillie, in the old country my cousin Loggia got life. How does one get five thousand years?"

"Oy, Theresa, do we have a lot to talk about!"

"*Mamma mia!* You are so right!"

5

KID MELNICK

Esther's first year in law school was going smoothly. She excelled in her studies and was working for Dean Lee.

This was a perfect fit for her, especially with complete access to the law library for her research.

Dean Lee asked Esther into his office. "Esther you have done so much for the Administration Office. Everything is running smoothly. I think you should have a little time for yourself. Why don't you take an elective course just to clear your head and have some fun? Maybe an art class?"

Esther was not impressed with the offer of an art class. Nevertheless, she knew he was correct because she was doing her schoolwork plus working at the office ten hours every day.

"Do you have a list of classes that I could attend?" Dean Lee walked to his desk and handed Esther a list of extracurricular and social club activities. She skimmed it. Something caught her eye and she started laughing.

Dean Lee, a very serious man, asked, "Esther may I ask what is making you laugh?"

"Oh, this is foolish, but I think I'd like to try learning the art of boxing. My older brother, Perry, was a good boxer in medical school. He even had several fights in the ring. Perry has a heavy bag still hanging in the garage at our house. I like this idea very much and I'll sign up and start boxing in summer school."

"Esther, there are some tough women in this class. Are you up for this?"

"My brother Perry was always punching me in my arms until the day I hit him back with my overhand right, the move he taught me when I was thirteen. He ran to tell Mama but he never hit me again."

"I'll make arrangements for you," the dean said, with just the barest hint of a smile. "The papers will be on your desk tomorrow morning."

"Thank you, Dean Lee. This will be fun and I do need to let off some steam."

What a gift boxing turned out to be for Esther! She took to it like a duck to water, excelling not only in boxing, but also in using her newfound talent in her legal research.

Esther was learning to jab, not only with her left hand, but also with knowledge for court, turning over every page looking for the opening, and executing the knockout blow.

On the bus home, Esther was feeling quite content with her life.

She was looking forward to some peaceful study time before a chaotic family dinner, which they experienced nightly.

Oh, the storytelling and kvetching that went on night after night! She loved every one of those dinners.

6

FALLING HARD

While studying in the living room, Esther was distracted by a knock at the door that changed her life forever.

She got up from her studies, walked to the front door, opened the small privacy window, and saw a young man.

"Hello, can I help you?"

The young man peered into the house.

"Good morning. I was told by Ben Siegel to meet Ben Melnick at this address. Mr. Melnick was to introduce me to his sister and said there would be a room for me to stay in while I'm studying law at John Marshall."

Esther was stunned by the thought of another person staying in her family's crowded home She quickly regained her composure, opened the front door, and found a handsome young man dressed in a suit, tie, and a smart hat.

"Really? This is news to me! What's your name?"

"Abraham Teitelbaum. Ben Melnick is a friend of my family in Brooklyn, and I believe this address is where I was to come. He asked, and what, pray tell, is your name?" Staring into the brownest eyes with the biggest twinkle, Esther was becoming curious about this stranger.

"I'm Esther Melnick! Mr. Teitelbaum, please wipe your shoes, take off your hat, and have a seat. I'll find my uncle Ben. He'll put an end to this mystery."

Esther ran up the stairs, turned, and peeked to check out Abraham's suit. She returned with Uncle Ben. Back at her studies, she was unable to concentrate. She wondered what would happen next.

7

OLD & NEW

Ben Melnick and Abraham Teitelbaum shook hands.

Ben, in a welcome of sorts, began. "Ben Siegel and Al Capone, my brother Felix, and even Johnny Torrio vouched for you. They said you were friends, that you worked for Johnny in Brooklyn."

Abe confirmed, "Yes, I was born just six blocks from Ben, in the same neighborhood as Al and Ralph Capone. They were older, but they took us under their wings."

Ben liked what he heard. He knew this would be of benefit to him in the long run, when his niece and this nice young man became attorneys.

Ben asserted, "A good reference is essential. I've been in business with Johnny Torrio since 1919. I'm his attorney, and attorney for the Capone family."

Abe was eager to impress Ben. Explained, "I know Johnny Torrio. He's another Brooklyn guy who made good with gambling and loan sharking. He did great business with those numbers! He's a smart man. Got started as a leader back in Brooklyn. Al Capone and Johnny worked at the same club. Al admired him and looked to him to be his mentor. Johnny was the nephew of Victoria Moresco, the wife and business partner of Big Jim Colosimo."

"He was the one who invited Johnny to come to Chicago to deal with extortion demands from the Black Hand. Johnny eliminated the extortionists and stayed on to run Big Jim's operations and to organize the criminal muscle that was needed to deal with threats."

"And then when Alphonse got in trouble by nearly beating to death a member of a rival operation, he was sent to Chicago to be a bouncer at one of Torrio's Chicago brothels but he soon became manager of the Four Deuces, one of Torrio's operations."

Ben replied, "Okay. Man, you're a talker and a history teacher! Get your damn luggage and I'll show you to your room. Remember, upstairs is off limits, except for family."

8

SEAL THE DEAL

"It's good you'll be attending John Marshall Law School. My niece, Esther, who you just met, is in her second year, working for Dean Lee as his law clerk. We'll talk more at dinner with my sister's family tonight."

Abe left his luggage in the small guest room on the first floor, put his clothes in order, and went back to the living room, where Esther was studying. He started to ask a question.

"Mr. Teitelbaum, I'm studying." She brushed him off, hoping to draw him closer.

"Please call me Abe. Let's not be formal. After all we're living in the same house and we should be friends. May I be so bold as to ask you: do you believe in love at first sight?"

"Abe, again, I'm working. Stop distracting me with silly talk. I'm working on a legal brief."

"Esther, I can help you if you'd just let me."

"Okay, smarty pants, leaf through this and tell me what doesn't apply."

A few minutes later Esther asked, impatiently, "Abe aren't you done yet?"

Smiling, Abe handed the paperwork back to her. "Listen, Esther. You'll hear what to do."

"Railroad commission of Wisconsin versus Chicago, B and Q. R. co.257 U.S. 563 (1922) The commission had investigated the interstate rates of carriers in the United States in a proceeding known as Ex Parte 74, increasing rates, 58. I.C.C 220 for the purpose of complying with 15A of the Interstate Commerce Act, as amended by 422 of the Transportation Act of 1920 (41 stat 448). That section requires the Commission to adjust rates that the revenues of the carriers shall enable, as a whole or by groups, to earn a fix net income on the railway property. The Commission ordered an increase for the carriers in the group of which the Wisconsin carriers were a part of 35% in interstate freight states, and 20% in interstate passenger fares, and excess baggage charges."

He smiled his most charming smile. Esther was stunned at the detailed response from this stranger in her home.

"Wow, Abe I see you have total recall, a very powerful tool for a lawyer!"

"Esther, I've always had the knack of remembering everything I read, but I suppose it's a gift, even though it feels perfectly natural. My true gift, however, is debriefing. Esther chuckled.

"Again I see you smiling!"

He was starting to feel his confidence rise.

"'Esther' is so formal. Could I call you Essie?"

He leaned a little more on the table, causing it to give way. Esther and Abe fell together on the floor. Abe ended up with his head resting in Esther's lap and they both laughed.

"Okay, Abe, I'll put up with you. You're piquing my interest."

"Essie, are you seeing anybody special?"

"Abe, I really don't have the time for this foolishness. I have to study."

"Ok, Essie, I'll take your answer as a no, so let's make a deal. We can study together and become buddies."

"Abe, you're charming and have a great mind. You've already proven that you can help me. I can help you. Will this be just you and me?"

"Essie, it will be just me and you. We'll be partners in school, and after the sun goes down, we'll be the best of friends."

Abe got up from the floor, helped Essie to her feet, and picked up all the papers.

Essie extended her hand. "Good deal, Mr. Teitelbaum! Let's shake on our new partnership."

"Shake? Miss Melnick, in mitigation, how about a kiss to seal the deal?" Esther, blushing, pulled Abe toward her.

"Okay, just to seal the deal."

At dinner, Esther introduced Abe to her family, who had many questions. This was becoming one of the longest family dinners that she'd ever experienced. The family wanted to know all about this young man who would be living with them. He tried his best to impress them.

They were a tough audience.

Morning came. Esther and Abe walked into the Admissions Office. Esther helped him to avoid the red tape that would have delayed his admission to law school.

Abe started law school, and this was the start of a very long love affair.

9

ANNULMENT

Esther was introduced to the Illinois Supreme Court by Dean Lee, and, thanks to his recommendation, was hired to clerk.

Due to her impeccable research, she was was in demand.

Gaining confidence daily, she met other attorneys and judges who she knew would become friends and resources.

After classes, Abe and Esther would walk to the deli, his favorite hangout. Abe took up their private time telling Esther more about his favorite subject: himself.

"Essie, the reason I left home was not just to go to law school. My parents forced me into an arranged marriage to a rich family friend. I ran away from this unconsummated marriage. Essie, would you please help me write an annulment that would legally free me to be with you?"

"Yes, I will. I have new friends in the courts and they'll help me to set you free. Unconsummated? Really? No matter, I truly don't want to know."

Esther did well, as always. The courts agreed. Abe's problem just went away.

10

GETTING PAID

Esther did not want to know that Abe had a dark side, but he felt the need to tell her some of his story.

"I was born in Brooklyn in 1906 and grew up in the same neighborhood as Ben Siegel and Al Capone, who was seven years older than us. Al and his brothers lived around the corner and up the block. Ben and I were just thirteen when we made friends with Ralph and Al. The next year Ralph introduced us to his cousin, Johnny Torrio. Johnny put us to work protecting his car while the older boys were cracking heads for the unions. We made contacts that would be beneficial when we needed them."

"One day we were running down the street to the Capones' home. Ralph and Al were sitting on the steps."

Ralph said, "Hey, it's the let's-knock-over-the-pushcart twins! What trouble are we doing today?' We told Al it was time for us to offer our talents to his mentor, Johnny Torrio, hoping he would have some work we could do besides causing havoc in the streets."

"Abe, how much more were you planning to tell me? I wasn't planning to listen to your whole life story tonight. Can we save some for tomorrow? You wore me out already." Abe looked at her with his big brown eyes and she knew she'd continue to listen for as long as he spoke.

"Essie, I'll finish up soon, I'm on a roll. Al and Ralph took us to see Johnny Torrio and we started the next week. Johnny picked us up and drove us to a huge commercial building where fifteen young men were gathered. The boys got paid five dollars each to get rid of scab workers for the union. He told them not to let anybody in the building. Ben and I guarded the car while the other boys went out behind Johnny to break some knees. Ben complained that the older guys were having fun until I reminded him we were getting paid."

"A year later Al and Ralph went to Chicago because the cops were breathing down their necks. Johnny had already gone to Chicago to work with Big Jim Colosimo, as his second-in-command of the South Side Gang. Johnny was flexing his muscles a little too much. Big Jim got nervous that Johnny was getting too ambitious and ordered a hit on him. You know the rest of the story because it involves your Uncle Ben. Esther, you look a little pale, and I guess I should wait till tomorrow for more. How about a little loving tonight?"

11

BIG BROADCAST

Esther had been attending boxing classes three days a week. Proficient at using her powerful overhand right, she could punch the heavy bag with authority.

In the summer of 1925, the Melnick family threw a Sunday party with friends and students from the local high schools and colleges. The captain of a Chicago university football team, a tall, strong, handsome young man, was talking to Esther, while looking down his nose at her.

"You must be kidding. Girls can't box. This is ridiculous!"

Abe interrupted, "Hey, big man, I'll wager $20 that Esther can give you a big time lesson in the fine art of pugilism."

"All right, Abe, I'll take your money but don't you worry. I'll just push her around for a couple of rounds."

Esther smirked while breaking out the boxing gear. She even helped the captain lace up his boxing gloves. She flirted a little by batting her sapphire blue eyes.

He seemed to be softening and that made her happy.

"Hope I didn't tie your gloves too tight. Is it true you're a football hero?"

"Damn it, Esther, I really don't want to hurt you. I'd like to take you out on a moonlit date."

"Captain, I can take care of myself. This'll be fun. By the way, did I mention I'm dating Abe? Can I bring him, too? Or maybe you'd be interested in my younger sister, Hannah? She's one hell of a winner. Talk to her about pitching coins."

Esther's younger sister, Hannah, was the referee for the event.

Esther's youngest brother, Alvin, now looking like Walter Winchell, had set up his amateur short wave radio on top of the garage with a table and chair, along with microphone, headset, and speakers, to broadcast the event to the neighborhood.

Abe was in Esther's corner. "Esther, listen. I think I have this shmuck figured out."

"Abe, hush. I've got this. Just relax and think where we're

going spend that money tonight. I'd like to go to a great dinner and paint the town red."

"Esther, kick his ass for me."

"Abe, stay close. This'll be over quickly."

Alvin Melnick was getting ready to broadcast, adjusting knobs for volume and drinking lemonade. The crowd was getting bigger and louder. Referee Hannah directed the crowd to form a big square. The whole neighborhood was pushing and shoving to get as close as they could to Kid Melnick. Alvin started the broadcast.

"Hello, Chicago, we're here on a beautiful sunny day, broadcasting on Alvin Melnick's radio station, sponsored by Ben Melnick, Attorney at Law. Just call Ben. He can fix anything, so call Sunnyside 5050. The fight is about to begin.

"In the blue corner we have Esther The Kid Melnick, 5 foot 3 inches at 135 pounds. In the red corner, the challenger, Hymie Rudnick, at 6 foot 1 inch, 185 pounds, the captain of the Chicago football team. Our referee for today is Hannah Melnick.

"And here we go! Hannah rings the bell for the first round, Kid Melnick ducks under a lazy punch, goes to work ripping a hard punch into the big man's gut, knocking the air out of him. Kid Melnick steps to the side and slams another hard left with authority right into his liver, bending him over. Wow! He's not so tall any more. Listen to the crowd going wild!

"Kid Melnick's giving the football hero a lesson he'll never forget! Holy Moly! Kid Melnick just threw her famous overhand right, knocking the captain to the ground, hard.

"Just listen to that crowd! The referee's counting. And, that's it! Kid Melnick is still unbeaten, 14 and 0."

The crowd is going wild as Abe Teitelbaum helps the loser to his feet.

"That's boxing for today, brought to you by our sponsor, Herman Melnick's Venetian Blind Shop on Clark Street, where shady is our business.

"Tune in next Sunday for me, Alvin Melnick, playing fiddle, with the Melnick sisters singing your favorite Western songs."

Abe collected $20 from the shaken football hero, and collected Esther The Kid Melnick, while the crowd yelled, "Three cheers for Kid Melnick!"

Esther's reputation as a boxer continued to spread until she graduated from law school. She hung up her gloves with a 16 and 0 record, with the exception of times when she needed to defend herself. Only then would she show her boxing skills.

12

THE DECISION

After the celebration of her big win, Esther's mama and Uncle Ben cornered her.

Esther knew about the type of clients Ben wanted her to defend. While in college, she had learned about what was going on in her city.

Johnny Torrio was returning to his apartment with his wife, Anna, when North Side gangsters Hymie Weiss, George "Bugs" Moran, and Vincent "The Schemer" Drucci met him and unloaded their guns. He survived, but just barely. Johnny decided for "health reasons" that it was a good time to hand over his South Side Gang to his protégé, Al Capone. Johnnie took off to Italy.

Esther was certain the future of the Outfit would continue to bring in Uncle Ben's friends as clients.

With mama's eyes on her, she knew she had to listen.

Uncle Ben lectured, "Esther, you can start your career as a low paid lackey for a big law firm where you will wait years and years for a few quality clients."

"Or, you can join me with your name on the shingle, from Day One, with guaranteed success. It's your choice but it would be foolish to pass up a golden opportunity that comes along only once in a lifetime."

"Look, Uncle Ben, I am already working for prestigious judges and they are quite pleased with my research. I think I will get a good job and well-paying clients not long after I graduate."

Esther wanted to be respected for the quality of her work and for her education. She had some of the best mentors in Chicago. She was fearful of what she would give up by working with Uncle Ben.

Mama was nodding her head. "Esther, listen to Uncle Ben. He has clients that pay very well and he can use your help. You will be successful in no time."

"I am giving it serious consideration, Mama. I will give you my answer right before graduation."

"That could be too late. Uncle Ben may have hired someone else by then."

"Please, Mama, let me get through school."

Uncle Ben delivered the final blow.

"Esther, we'll put your boyfriend's name on the shingle, too, when he graduates. It will read: Melnick, Melnick, and Teitelbaum."

Esther's mother was intent on her joining Uncle Ben and was relentless in pressuring her.

Esther thought about Abe and wanted to secure his future. She enjoyed daydreaming about working with Abe toward building a life together.

Reluctantly, she agreed to join Uncle Ben, although fearful that she would regret this decision for the rest of her life.

In 1927, Esther and Abe graduated from John Marshall Law School.

They became partners in Uncle Ben's law firm. Esther did the research, sending Abe to do the court appearances.

(In 1928, Esther took a case to the United States Supreme Court: The United States of America, Ex Rel. Carl Silver, Petitioner, Versus Thomas O'Brien, Sheriff of Cook County, Illinois, Attorney Esther Melnick. She won the right for homeowners to not be thrown out of their homes without due process.)

Uncle Ben became more interested in betting on the ponies than in doing his legal work, which he was leaving up to Abe. Ben started losing money. Esther, at her mother's insistence, kept paying off the debts. It was ironic that, with his connections, he could lose so much money.

13

FOR OLD TIME'S SAKE

Ralph Capone, with two of his thug collectors, visited the office.

"Ben, you now owe us $30,000. I promise you this: you have until Monday to pay or you'll feel the pain."

Ralph said this calmly, but his eyes conveyed sinister sincerity.

Ben acted insulted. "Ralph, you know me. Have I ever failed to settle up with you or Al?"

Ralph's response was simple. "Let me show you what we're gonna do."

Ralph waved and pointed at the 6th floor window. Within seconds, his collectors grabbed Ben's legs and had him hanging out the window. Ralph and collectors laughed and taunted him, threatening to drop him. They let him dangle for about a minute.

Abe Teitelbaum entered the office. Seeing his partner hanging from the window, he demanded that they pull Esther's uncle up into the room.

"Jesus, Ralph, that's Esther's mom's brother! You know this'll cause a shit storm if Tillie calls your mama. We really don't want this. Whatever Ben did, we can work this out. Pull his ass back into the building, for old time's sake."

Ralph hesitated for a second and grinned at Abe. "Ok, boys, haul in the fish." Laughing, they pulled Ben back from the abyss.

Ben was speechless. Once in the safety of the office, it became obvious that he had pissed on himself. He crawled to the nearest wastebasket, leaned his head in, and puked.

"Ben, you've only got till next Monday. If it wasn't for Abe, you would've been on the pavement. You don't have Johnny Torrio to protect you any more. Just pay the fucking money or feel the pain! You're one lucky shmuck. Oh, by the way, say hello to Esther for me. Too bad she wasn't here."

Ralph Capone laughed as he and his muscle exited the front door.

Esther returned to the office. Ben was in a state of shock, still shaking.

"Ben, what's wrong? You look sick. Need a seltzer?"

"No, Esther, I don't need a seltzer! I need to change my pants. I also need thirty thousand dollars to give to Ralph's collectors before next Monday or I'm a dead man. If it wasn't for Abe they would've tossed me out the window, and to top it all off, Ralph said to say hello to you."

Esther, disgusted, snapped, "Listen to me, Buster. I'm not your mama. God damn it! You got yourself into this mess, now you get yourself out! I'm not going to pay any more of your gambling debts. I paid them for the last time! I don't care what Mama says any more. Thirty thousand dollars is insanity! This is your problem. Now go talk your way out of this one and make a deal."

"Esther, I need to pay the vig at the very least. It'll give me another week to deal. All I need is five thousand to buy me another week."

Ben was crying, begging on his knees, and scared to the bone. He knew the Capones didn't mess around. Their word was gold and he was the object of their word.

Esther gave Ben the five thousand from her desk. "I want you to know this is my money that I'm giving you, mine and mine alone. Ben, listen carefully! There will be no more. This is the last time."

"God bless you, Esther. I'll do whatever it takes. This will never happen again."

Esther shook her head, knowing that Ben was lying.

Because of her mama and her family loyalty, Esther had always looked the other way and didn't get involved in Ben's business. It was becoming too much to ask.

14

FAMILY DANGER

That night, Ben packed everything he owned that was of value. Before leaving, he called his brother Felix in New York City. Ben told him he was in a lot of trouble with Ralph and the Outfit and had to leave town fast. He was worried that this may be it, and he could be a dead man. He didn't have Johnny Torrio to protect him any more.

Loyalty was really out the window these days.

Felix, not surprised, merely asked, "Ben, what the fuck did you do this time?"

"I had a solid tip that Tag the Runner was going to win the fifth race at Hawthorne. I was told to bet the farm. My source was always reliable, Felix. I don't know what happened. The horse pulled up lame going around the last turn. The nag finished last."

"I bet thirty grand I didn't have. Now the bookies and the Capone brothers are looking to get paid. I don't have the fucking money. I'm thinking Toronto might be the answer. We went there on the lam before. I don't know what else to do."

"Well, Ben, I can't get you the money. I simply don't have it."

Felix was no help, but Esther's five grand would be enough to get him to Canada, change his name, and set him up.

Ben left Chicago once again. He didn't care that he was leaving his family, his law firm, and his only sister holding the bag. He didn't care that he put them all in danger. He left to protect his own skin.

The Chicago Outfit's collectors knocked on the Melnicks' door on Clark Street, demanding that the family pay off the debt or be thrown into the street, losing their business. Herman went to the door.

"Tillie, who are these people? Why do we owe anything to anybody? Aren't these Ben's friends?"

"Look, old man! Ben worked for us. He lost thirty thousand dollars! He was living here and you're related to him. You'll pay us the money or we'll take over your business and your home. We will be coming back. Remember, you have until next Monday. You need to have every penny."

"Okay, it's time for you to leave. We heard your message," Tillie commanded, unshaken. "It's time for you messenger boys to get out of my house and don't you ever come back again!"

No one had talked to these two thugs like this before. They looked in disbelief at this small, crippled woman who had the confidence of one of their bosses. The two turned to the door and left in silence.

Tillie called her friend, Theresa Capone. They arranged a meeting with Esther, Abe, Teresa, and Alphonse and Ralph Capone at the law office on Clark Street.

15

DANCING ON THE RAZOR'S EDGE

"It's not the thing you fear that you must deal with: it is the mother of the thing you fear."

- David Whyte

At the meeting, Tillie, spoke first. "Theresa, you're my friend. My brother is in trouble. I know if the situation were reversed and Al or Ralph were in trouble with Ben, I would help you make a deal."

"Tillie, this ain't none of your business," Ralph interrupted. "Ben owes us a great deal of money for a stupid bet he made without having the cash to back it up. We just want to get paid."

Theresa Capone was lecturing her two sons. "Shame on you

Ralph. Sending goons to Tillie's house is just wrong. In the old country, the responsible one had to pay up, not his sister or niece. You and Al have it all wrong. Look, my sweet boys, these people are our friends."

"How many scrapes have Abe and Esther gotten you out of? Now you want to pick on Esther's mother for a few dollars?"

"Al," Abe interjected, "Ben has left for places unknown. I suspect his brother Felix knows, but you know Felix. He's so tight-lipped, he has to drink whiskey through a cocktail straw. He'll never reveal where Ben is. So my question is, how do we fix this problem?"

Al Capone turned to Abe and Esther. "Here's the deal. We don't want to lose you as our lawyers, but Ben is through. As far as we're concerned, he's a nobody now. We'll make sure he's disbarred, that he's never again going to represent another human being. We'll ruin him, financially. He'll be lucky to get three meals a day. If he ever returns to Chicago, I will personally kill him and Ralph will watch as I cut out his tongue and gouge out his eyes before I shoot him in his head. Ben is dead to my outfit and me. Nothing he can do will ever change that."

"Like I said, Abe, we want you and Esther to represent us. We'll continue to send you others that we trust to be your clients. Ben's name, of course, comes off the firm's name. We also want you to move your office to Cicero, where we're headquartered. You can keep the downtown office for court and stuff like that, but I want to be able to walk across the street for legal advice. You get my drift here?"

A deal was made to erase Uncle Ben's debt to the Chicago Outfit: Ben's name came off the law firm, shortening it to Melnick & Teitelbaum.

Abe and Esther became the Capone family's attorneys. Ralph closed the book on Ben's losses. The deal included a fifty thousand dollar cash payment to Esther to move the firm to a more convenient location and to hire a private bodyguard, Louis Romano, to whom they would pay $30,000 a year.

Louis had been working for Alphonse as his driver and bodyguard for the past three years. It was time for Louis to start making connections by working for Esther and Abe. This would ensure the Capones' privacy, and give status to this very smart young man who would become good friends with his bosses, Esther and Abe.

They learned to trust him. Louis' status changed. He now had his own bodyguard.

(A few years later, in 1934, Louis was promoted to president of the Chicago Bartenders Union, at the same time that Abe became president of the Chicago Restaurant Union.)

After Tillie and Theresa left the office, Al Capone talked privately with Esther and Abe.

"When me and Ben were getting paid for the union work we were doing, times were great. We had fun, made some money. Life was like a constant party. When Ralph and me moved to Chicago, well, I had the desire to be at the top, the boss, not some flunky working for the boss. When Ben introduced my mother to Esther's mother, a great family friendship was created. It's that family friendship, the personal bond, that caused me to take the heat off Ben. If he ever discovers what happened, then Abe, I will kill you dead. I'm not kidding here. Keep that fucking Ben Melnick away from me and never tell him just how close he came to meeting his maker. I never want to see the prick again. Let him rot wherever he is. I curse Ben Melnick!"

Al put out the word to everyone that he wanted Ben Melnick blackballed and penniless. He told his friends to spread the word.

With all the business taken care of, Al and Ralph left the office. Abe was excited about what he saw as their good fortune, planning to get himself into the limelight as the fixer.

Esther was starting to worry that this new venture would go to Abe's head. She warned, "Abe, don't be dreaming about the limelight. It's better to be in the back in the dark, pulling strings, than in the light where everyone knows our business. That could be dangerous for both of us."

"Honey, don't worry. We have Louis to protect us and he ain't a cowboy. He's one serious man, who now jumps just for us."

Esther felt conflicted. When she started law school, She had planned to practice to help the downtrodden.

That ideal had its origin many years ago, when she was born into a large family where she learned the value of selfless caring.

Now she rationalized that, although the socially acceptable clientele she had daydreamed about was absent, the unsavory clients that she did have needed her help just as much.

That was okay for now.

16

OUTFIT: 14, ESTHER: 0

Esther, wrestling with her plight, answered the phones. She told prospective clients that their retainer would be $125,000 per year, thinking that this would discourage the criminal element from hiring them.

What happened was shocking to her: everyone who contacted the firm came in with the cash.

Whoever said, "crime doesn't pay" must have read the wrong book!

Remembering Abe's excitement over betting on her boxing matches, she worried that he might lose their money like Uncle Ben did.

She squirreled away cash in her hatboxes and hired her sister,

Hannah, to work for their law firm. She knew she could trust Hannah with everything from information about clients to their money.

17

PAPERS OUTRAGED

On January 27, 1929, Ralph Capone picked up Abe for a three-week trip to Alphonse's residence at 93 Palm Drive, Miami Beach, Florida.

Al's neighbors were wailing that the Capones were becoming a nuisance, what with people coming and going at all hours of the day and night. Loud parties and shady sorts (the fedora over the face crowd) were invading their nice, quiet neighborhood.

On their first day in Florida, Al took Abe to visit his personal tailor, where Abe was fitted for new suits, shirts, and ties. Alphonse wanted to be sure that his personal attorney looked as snorky as he did. (Al Capone wanted to be called Snorky to reinforce his image as a successful businessman).

The suits and shirts were ready in record time, with not one fitting needed. They were perfect for the lunch meetings that Al and Abe would attend with the Dade County District Attorney.

At these meetings, Al said nothing, letting Abe be his mouthpiece.

In the evenings, Al threw loud parties for those neighbors who were not giving him a hard time. The Dade County District Attorney was Al's honored guest every evening.

The last meeting was held on February 13, 1929, during which they were informed that the neighbors' complaints had been withdrawn.

The D.A. said with a sly grin, "Al, I convinced those complainers that you had a right to privacy on your own property, that the estate was large enough to accommodate many guests, that as long as the guests are acting within the laws of Florida and Dade County, there was nothing they could do. I even suggested that they apologize to you for being so testy. I told them they would probably get an invite to a party. That seemed to do the trick."

The next day, the prosecuting attorney from Brooklyn, who was vacationing in Florida, met with Abe and Al after learning that Al was recovering from a sore throat. After talking with Abe, he left to go back to Brooklyn. Capone and

Abe went to the pool to enjoy the sun and take a break from the Windy City's snow.

February 14, 1929, Valentine's Day, will always be remembered in Chicago as the day when seven members of "Bugs" Moran's North Side Gang were brutally murdered.

The papers were outraged by the orgy of bloodshed in the garage used by Moran's gang. The headlines called this gangland killing "The Saint Valentine's Day Massacre."

It was sad day for Chicago.

Meanwhile, back at 93 Palm Drive, Miami Beach, Florida, Al Capone was with his attorney, Abe Teitelbaum, taking in the sun.

Al was in Florida for three weeks, not only with Abe, but also with many attorneys from Dade County. On this fateful day, even the vacationing prosecuting attorney from Brooklyn who was visiting, was witness to his whereabouts.

Al Capone had an airtight alibi for the Saint Valentine's Day massacre.

When Abe returned to Chicago, he found that Esther had moved them into the New Drake Hotel Apartments. He had with him four suitcases full of new clothes.

"Abe, what's with all the luggage?" Esther asked. "You left with one small suitcase and come back with four?"

"Alphonse had twelve suits made special for me, and a blue tuxedo, two dozen shirts and ties."

"That was very generous of him, excluding that you were his alibi. You were with him for the last three weeks."

"Essie, Alphonse didn't have anything to do with Moran's boys getting knocked off. We were at the District Attorney's office, fighting his neighbors' complaints, when that happened."

"I don't want to know. The newspapers are digging for dirt, and it's not going to be easy to avoid getting crap splattered on you. Once it's there, it's hard to wash out."

"Essie, let's leave the shit out of this conversation."

A master of distraction, Abe turned the conversation to a new subject.

"I have some good news. Capone opened an account at Marshall Field's for you. He told me to let you get everything you want, and to make sure you get a full-length mink coat. You can thank him when we have dinner on Friday."

18

PUBLIC OPINION

Abe and Esther were escorted to a private dining area at The Continental Hotel.

Alphonse walked in with Ralph and the bodyguards, who were seated at the table next to the door. Esther was tired from the long workweek but she was dressed to the nines, sporting her new mink coat and a beautiful hat with bird feathers.

She felt Al's eyes on her and this made her uncomfortable. She knew things were getting more complicated by the day. Alphonse gave her the once over and smiled approvingly. "Not only are you smart, but beautiful, too. I can't believe one of the pushcart twins could be so lucky. Speaking of the twins, Ben Siegel will be here in a few minutes to join us. He's taking care of a little business for me."

Abe and Esther perked up. They hadn't seen Ben in a while, and Ben always enjoyed catching up with what was happening in Atlantic City and California.

Ben was running with the Hollywood crowd and always had great stories to tell. Esther was happy to see Ben. His stories were more interesting and fun than Alphonse's legal problems, which were mounting daily. Since the Valentine's Day Massacre.

Alphonse's thinly veiled alibi had undermined his carefully built reputation. He was falling out of favor with the newspapers, and especially with public opinion.

19

BAIT & SWITCH

In early August 1931, Judge Wilkerson called the Federal Prosecutor, George E. O. Johnson, and the Capone tax attorney, Lawrence Mattingly, plus Alphonse Capone, into his chambers.

"Boys, this has been going on long enough. We have been selecting a jury for the last month, and we're nearly there. I know negotiations on Mr. Capone's behalf have taken place. George, I know you believe that you'll have trouble with your star witness. Mr. Mattingly, your client is on the hook for anywhere from two to twenty-five years. I want no hanky-panky in this trial. You will control your client or there will be hell to pay. Let me make this perfectly clear: negotiations in my courtroom are few and far between, especially with a defendant with the notoriety of Mr. Capone. The trial will begin as soon as the last juror is selected. There will be no bargaining in my courtroom. Is that clear?"

Mattingly asked, "Your Honor, may I have a few minutes with my client to discuss the situation?"

"Of course. You may use the Jury Room. The door is unlocked."

Mattingly and Capone whispered in the Jury Room. "Al, this doesn't look so good."

"Look, Mattingly, I just want this to go away. I can do two or three years standing on my head."

"I think the judge might just might accept that."

Mattingly quickly wrote a note suggesting that Capone would plead guilty to a single charge in exchange for two years in a federal prison.

The pair slowly walked back to Judge Wilkerson's chambers. Upon entering, they noticed a court reporter with his stenotype machine poised at the ready.

"What's this?" Mattingly demanded, outraged.

"I thought you might come back with some kind of guilty plea. I want any conversation to this effect to be on the record."

"Okay with me," George Johnson offered.

"Your honor, Mr. Capone would consider pleading guilty... well, I have it all here in this note."

Mattingly handed the hastily penned note to the judge.

20

A FOUL ODOR

Alphonse and Ralph Capone, along with three bodyguards, marched into the law office.

"Hi boys," said Hannah, "Esther and Abe are in with your tax attorneys. Why all the extra hardware?"

Ralph changed the subject. "Hannah, do you mind if my boys stay in your waiting room while I sit in with the Teitelbaums and my brother? Maybe show the boys how to pitch coins?"

Hannah responded with faked authority, "No problem, Ralph."

In her most sultry voice, Hannah, said, "Hello boys. Anybody want to pitch coins or play craps or just have a cup of coffee?"

Al and Ralph stepped into the office. The attorneys were in a serious conversation. Abe was talking to Mattingly.

"Why in the world would you give the court a letter with an offer in writing to plead guilty? Esther and I would never have done that in federal court. You first let the court show its hand, and then you negotiate, you put the cart before the horse, possibly causing grievous damage to your client."

Mattingly explained, "I've been negotiating with the federal prosecutors for over five months. Finally, they asked me what Alphonse would be willing to do to end this process. I then, by hand, wrote what I felt would satisfy the government and would be agreeable to Mr. Capone."

"Without consulting your client?" Abe asked, in disbelief.

"No, Al was there."

Attorney Michael Ahern interrupted. "Mattingly wrote the offer and gave it to the judge. He was in agreement with the judge and the federal prosecutor to allow Alphonse to plead to a lesser charge and get a year or two. This all seemed reasonable. No one ever got more than eighteen months for tax evasion, like Frank Nitti, and now he's out."

Ahern produced a letter and handed it to Abe, who quickly read it, passed it to Esther, and asked, "How bad is this?"

Esther read the letter and became angry. "My advice is that

we get a thirty day postponement. Abe and I should be able to go in and negotiate a real deal for you. Alphonse, your 'tax' attorneys don't have the court deal in writing. What they're offering you is nothing but a bait and switch and it will emit a foul odor in the end. I've seen this in court before and the judge will throw the book at you. Please don't listen to this nonsense. What I see here is that your tax attorneys are pleading you guilty before any real negotiations."

Esther vented her anger. "Mattingly, you wasted five months! The court tripped you up with sleight of hand, using an amateur trick. It seems to me that you have no concern for your client. Alphonse, do you understand you can be put away for twenty years without even a radio?"

Alphonse announced confidently, "Ralph dropped thousands of dollars to six members of the jury and it will be just another day in court."

Esther shook her head and bit her lip. "Alphonse, why are you rushing through this? Let's get an easy thirty-day postponement. I'll do all the research until I find the loopholes in the government's case, including voiding Mattingly's letter. In case the judge goes rogue, we can use the law to force the court to agree with us."

Alphonse told Esther he wanted all this to go away as quickly as possible, again assuring her that six jurors were paid off. He wanted to take his chances. He felt confident that the money he spread around would, as usual, get him what he wanted.

Ralph was not convinced that Al was making sense. He was worried and felt it would be better to have all twelve of the jury in their pocket. He reminded Alphonse, "Esther and Abe have never lost a case for the family."

Ralph couldn't convince Alphonse to listen.

He shouted his favorite line, "Ralph, I know what I'm doing!"

They left the office with the three bodyguards. All had long faces.

Alphonse glanced at Hannah. "Did you clean my boys out of their pocket money?"

Hannah was popping her gum. "Just a hundred and twenty bucks. The boys can come back any time to get even. I have very famous gambling partners, including Mickey and Ben. I just seem to have beginner's luck over and over again."

"Hannah, does anybody besides me know that you're a ringer?"

Esther chimed in, "She taught me to throw leaners when she was just a child. Let me give you some advice: never pitch coins with Hannah!"

Al had a smile on his face for the first time all day. He had a soft spot for Hannah. She seemed so innocent, and sharp as a tack.

He waved to everyone to leave the office and asked Hannah, "Did Esther hit Mickey in the arm and make him whine?"

Hannah laughed. "I will never tell what goes on in this office. Esther trained me well to never talk about our clients, so I can neither confirm nor deny what actually happened."

She winked and Alphonse smiled again.

21

"YOU HAVE NOT SEEN THE LAST OF ME"

On June 30, 1931, the bailiff read the indictments in Judge Wilkerson's Court. "Three felony tax evasion counts for 1925, 1926, and 1928, and two failure-to-file misdemeanor counts for the years 1928 and 1929."

Just as Esther had feared, the risks of Mattingly's deal were about to be realized.

This morning, in open court, Alphonse's tax attorneys, Ahern, Mattingly, and Fink, sat with him at the bench in front of an angry judge.

"There will be no bargaining in my court. You can now take Alphonse's guilty plea and toss it in the trash where it belongs. Mr. Capone, you will get your day in court."

Mattingly had foolishly led Alphonse to believe that it was a done deal, agreed to by the federal prosecutor and the judge. Such was never the case. The carelessly penned offer of a guilty plea was never considered by him and may have even prejudiced the judge, into rendering a harsher sentence than was the required minimum.

Al, picturing Esther's face in his mind, heard the judge say, "Trial will begin tomorrow. Have your witnesses ready. I expect brief opening statements."

Just before the trial started, federal marshals informed Judge Wilkerson that there was evidence of jury tampering.

The first jury placed in another courtroom, and the new jury was paraded into Judge Wilkerson's courtroom.

The trial of Alphonse Capone began with many objections from both sides. Judge Wilkerson would have none of the legal maneuvering. Several witnesses on each side were called to testify.

Most of the judge's rulings with regard to the many objections raised by the defense were in favor of the prosecution. There were so many that it became prudent to keep a log of those rulings that the defense saw as prejudicial to their client.

The trial went on longer than Al Capone and his attorneys had expected.

On October 17, 1931, Al Capone, out on bail, was at the

Lexington Hotel when he received a phone call saying that the jury was in. A verdict had been reached. Al and Ralph, along with their bodyguards, rushed to the District Court.

Al Capone and his lawyers filed into the crowded courtroom and were seated on the left side.

Esther and Abe Teitelbaum were sitting quietly behind the division. Esther was holding Abe's hand.

The bailiff sounded, "All rise! The District Court of the United States of America for the Northern District of Illinois, Eastern Division, is now in session United States versus Alphonse Capone. All parties come forward and be heard. Judge James Wilkerson presiding."

"Be seated. Good afternoon. Has the jury reached a verdict?"

The jury foreman stood up and said, "Yes, Your Honor, we have."

The bailiff walked over to the jury and was handed a folded piece of paper. He gave it to Judge Wilkerson, who examined the verdict and handed it to the court clerk, who gave it back to the jury foreman.

"Please read the verdict."

"On indictment number 22852 for the year 1924, we find the defendant not guilty. On indictment number 23232 for the years 1925, 1926, 1927, 1928, and 1929, we find the defendant guilty."

There was a commotion as reporters rushed out of the courtroom to report the guilty verdict.

Judge Wilkerson struck his gavel. "I will fine anyone $100 for charging out of this courtroom! Everyone take your seats! Mr. Capone and attorneys, please rise."

Alphonse Capone and his attorneys stood.

The judge continued, "Alphonse Capone, you will appear on October 24th for sentencing."

Al knew that he should have listened to Esther. He could control himself no longer.

"You have not seen the last of me!"

On the 24th of October, Esther and Al were listening to the radio.

Breaking news! Alphonse Capone returned to court for sentencing today. He was sentenced to eleven years in federal penitentiary and was fined $50,000. He was ordered to pay court costs totaling $30,000. Capone had been convicted on five felony counts and two misdemeanors. The misdemeanor charges of failure to file a tax return added one year to the sentence. He was handcuffed and taken away.

Just like that, Alphonse Capone went to prison. His rule of the Chicago Mob ended. He never regained the position of power that he had owned like a king.

In the long run, that hit on business meant little to Abe and Esther Teitelbaum. Their clientele of leaders of organized crime continued to grow.

Al Capone's incarceration was merely a bump in the road.

22

FIRM WITH INFLUENCE

Esther and Abe remained the attorneys for Al's family and for the Outfit.

The Melnick and Teitelbaum law firm was now located in the Fine Arts Building on Michigan Avenue, behind the Buckingham Fountain. Abe bought twenty percent of the building, including the private stairwell to the tenth floor. The tenth floor became the firm's headquarters. The building contained many offices for the arts. His purchase included one-third of the theater, as well.

In 1932, Abe's specialty was labor negotiations. He was appointed chief counsel to the Chicago Restaurant Association, with the assistance of the Chicago Outfit.

Louis Romano was appointed president of the Bartenders

Association. Together, Abe and Louis controlled six service associations.

Esther now had her own law library. She did all the research for the firm, while Abe, using his total recall, went to court and won cases.

23

ITALIAN ADVENTURE

Things were not always smooth. Abe's mother and sister were constantly causing trouble for the Melnick family.

The final insult came when Abe was needed in Italy to settle a paralyzing workers' strike. Abe's mother and sister booked passage on the same cruise ship and traveled with Abe during the two months he was gone. Esther was furious. When he finally arrived home she gave him an earful.

"Abe, your mother and sister have been trying to sabotage our wedding plans for years. They went to Europe with you just to cause me grief!"

Abe hugged her. His smile always melted her heart, even when she wanted to give him a left to the liver.

Abe tried to soothe Esther.

"Please, Essie, please calm down. My mother and sister just wanted to show me around when I wasn't working. And don't forget, this trouble goes way back to your parents being so uppity, always talking down to my family. Let's just say that the fault is shared. Remember, the deal I made to settle the labor strike will be very good for us. Did you get the wire from the Italian government for the $200,000? Oh, and by the way, the Italian government shipped us a beautiful, huge desk. It should arrive at our office soon."

A bit calmer now, Essie said, "Yes, Abe, I got the wire. That's not what I'm talking about. I put up with the insults because they are your family."

"I can't take this any more. I don't mind our parents butting heads, but your mom and sister were trying to break us up while you were gone. I was informed that your sister tried to match you up with a rich family's daughter in Poland!"

Abe joked, "True, but the girl had one eye, a big nose and a huge tush!"

He gave her another hug. "Essie, there's nothing they can do to break us up. The wedding is planned for next month and that's when we'll tie the knot, period!"

That's what she'd always wanted to hear, that he was going to make their relationship permanent.

A telegram was delivered to the office for Abe. It was from his mother and sister and said, "Do you have to marry that woman?"

Esther showed him this nasty telegram.

"Abe, This telegram is the last straw. I'm just so tired of their interference in our lives."

It was true that she was tired; she had enough on her plate with researching all the cases and filling in for him in court. She was so tired that she was not thinking straight. Abe embraced her.

"Essie, please let it go. I am absolutely certain they are not going to be at our wedding next month."

24

THE MERGER

Esther refused to let Abe get away that easily. She told him he'd better propose properly and get down on one knee.

"Esther, I have always told you that I fell hard for you on the first day we met, so long ago on Clark Street. Dear Miss Esther Melnick, will you please marry me as soon as possible? Now let's get a pastrami sandwich to seal the deal."

Esther desperately wanted this marriage. She wanted to merge her law partnership and her personal life into a single bond. She even agreed to his favorite way of celebrating anything: a pastrami sandwich.

They held hands while they walked to the deli for a sandwich and a two cents plain.

The bonds were cemented when Esther and Abe married on July 19, 1932.

On the way to Crown Point, Indiana, Abe ran a red light and was pulled over by a motorcycle cop. The officer demanded that Abe produce a license and asked if he knew why he was being stopped.

Abe, not wanting Esther to get angry for making them late, told the officer, "Yes, Sir, I ran a red light." The officer mounted his motorcycle and waved Esther and Abe to follow him to the courthouse. Esther worried that this was a bad omen. Abe assured her that he would handle it.

Judge Edelman presided over the traffic court. "Mr. Abraham Teitelbaum, you have been arraigned here today for passing a red light. How do you plead?"

Abe was feeling lucky on his wedding day. With his most charming voice he replied, "Your Honor, I did run through the stop light, however, in mitigation I would say I was on my way to Crown Point, Indiana with Miss Esther Melnick, Esq. We are to be married today."

"That being the case, not guilty! I'm going to give you the green light, along with a police officer to escort you to the state line at Crown Point. This will be my court's wedding present to the both of you. Good luck. Officer, do as I have instructed. Case dismissed!"

Abe flashed his biggest smile and replied, "Thank you, Your Honor." Esther whispered that he never ceased to amaze her.

Esther and Abe were married, as reported in the Chicago Herald Examiner. They spent their honeymoon in New York City.

The connections to New York City and Chicago became intertwined, creating a new standard of dealing with labor relations, under the tutelage of the young lawyers, Esther and Abe Teitelbaum.

The Teitelbaums saw their law practice booming by the end of 1932. They brought in many new clients, each of whom paid $125,000 in retainers per year.

The sky was the limit.

25

FOIA LIST

The following information was gathered by the Federal Bureau of Investigation, and revealed to me through the Freedom of Information Act.

Known associates and clients of Esther and Abraham 1928 to 1960:

Johnny Torrio, Benjamin Siegel, Allen Smiley, Theresa Capone, Alphonse Capone, Ralph Capone, Tony Accardo, Louis Campagna, Philip D'Andrea, Charles Gioe, Paul Ricca, Moses Annenberg, The Chicago Bartenders Association, Joe Isca, Los Angeles Teamsters Union, Nate Dubow, Chicago Restaurant Association, Harry Winston, Church of the Latter Day Saints, Jimmy Durante, Sands Hotel, Riviera Hotel, Gene Autry, Ben Swig, Senior Pritzer, Hacienda Corporation, Jake Guzik, Meyer Lansky, Desert Inn, Ramada

Inn, Johnny Dio, Jack Dragna, Tom Dragna, Jimmy Fratianno, Van Cleef & Arpels, Mickey Cohen, Harry Teitelbaum, Murray Humphreys, Sidney Korshak, Louis Romano, Johnny Roselli, Louis Cowen, Sam Giancana, Joe Pasternak, Salvatore "Lucky" Luciano, MGM Studios, Abner "Longie" Zwillman, Paramount Studios, Arrington Hotel, Universal Studios, Columbia Studios, Greater Chicago Hotel Association, Edgewater Beach Hotel, Steinway Drug Stores, John R. Thompson Restaurants, Chicago Candy Association, Toffenetti Triangle Restaurants.

With a client list like this, Esther and Abe were doing quite well. Money was no object.

The pair was rolling in dough.

26

BIG YELLOW TAXI

Esther and Abe dined out on Michigan Avenue almost every evening.

One night, after a wonderful dinner with Judge Green and his wife, they ordered a Yellow Cab to take them back to the Drake. The night was cold and snow was lightly falling.

Ads on the Yellow Cab doors promised that they would take you to your destination safely. Abe and Esther trusted the company to take them on this short trip.

On this night, the driver ran a light and was hit by another car in the intersection. Esther and Abe were thrown around in the back seat and Esther hit the floor. She blacked out.

"Oh, Essie, are you all right?" He kissed her on the forehead.

Esther, groggy, opened her beautiful eyes and told Abe she was in pain.

"Relax, Essie, we're getting an ambulance to take you to the hospital."

"Oh, Abe, we don't have time for this." She lost consciousness once again.

Esther was in the hospital for a couple of weeks. Luckily, her neck was not broken but she needed traction. After being discharged, she was quickly back to work.

From that time forward, Esther was always in pain. She could not look left or right without wincing. Abe filed a lawsuit against the Yellow Cab Company and they received a large settlement.

"I'm happy to have our settlement but I don't think that's enough. I want the cab company to take that reassuring slogan off their doors. They certainly did not get us anywhere safely."

27

CHICAGO FIXER

With Abe Teitelbaum firmly in control of the Chicago Restaurant Association as Chief Counsel and President, and Louis Romano in absolute control of the Chicago Bartenders Union, Abe was now in control of six labor associations. Life was getting more and more exciting, but more complicated, as well.

The law firm was defending fourteen top members of the Chicago Outfit, and it was successful in each case.

Esther did the research until she found loopholes. In court, Abe used his knowledge to set the guilty free.

28

CALIFORNIA'S NEWEST ATTORNEY

Esther's introduction to the life of Benjamin Siegel was Abe's story about standing on the corner of Jackson and Michigan Avenues. When Abe reached into his pocket for his wallet, he found himself shaking hands with his childhood friend, Ben, ever the joker!

Abe went to Los Angeles to meet with Ben, who had taken over the L.A. Teamsters Union and was busy controlling Mickey Cohen and the Dragna brothers.

The Dragna brothers were taking over some of the film industry unions in order to extort and influence the movie studios.

Ben loved that limelight, and loved mixing with stars and studio heads.

He took money from his Mob-struck fans for various business deals. Instead of paying them back he would show up at their events and dinner parties. That seemed to do the trick. Ben took $200,000 from a Beverly Hills doctor to partner in a piece of prime property. He never intended to buy the property or pay him back.

The doctor's son, who resembled Abe, could not pass his law exams. Ben hooked him up with Abe, who came to town and took the young man's law exam for him. It helped that Abe looked like the young man in size and weight.

Of course, Abe passed the test.

Esther was not thrilled with this idea. She worked hard and studied diligently to get her law degree. Here was Abe, getting this young man out of taking the exam at all by standing in.

The young man became a partner in a prestigious Beverly Hills law firm in only three months. In seven years, he was appointed to the Superior Court. Fifteen years later he was appointed to the highest court in California.

"Abe, it's great to have a judge in a high place, and one who must return favors for many years," said Ben, slapping Abe on the back.

"Esther will have to admit, it's good to have judges you can ask favors of."

29

STRIFE, TROUBLE, & CASH

Abe spent a lot of time in California. He stayed at the Beverly Hills Hotel.

There was trouble between the Dragna brothers and Mickey Cohen. It escalated like a slow-boiling pot: a little push, a small grab from Mickey, and a push back from the brothers, until one night at Mickey's home in Brentwood, the pot boiled over.

Someone planted a bomb that blew off the front door and then spent a few seconds shooting up the house. Mickey was hopping mad and called Abe to see the damage first-hand. Just as the police were leaving, Abe got out of his car He walked up the path to Mickey's house. There was no front door. Mickey and his bodyguards appeared at the gaping hole.

Mickey told the cops it must have been a gas leak. The police investigators knew that the house was severely damaged by gunfire. After taking it all down in notes, they offered protection, which was promptly refused.

A few days later, Abe spoke to Esther on the phone, long distance.

"Esther, this was the conversation: 'Good morning, Mickey, I didn't know you were remodeling.' Mickey made the prune face then said 'Dammit, this is not funny. I'm pissed off! Look at my new suit hanging on my coat rack. I paid 400 dollars and never wore it and it's burnt to a crisp. I want those brothers on a hook.' Then I asked Mickey if he was more upset about the suit or the house."

"I realized this was turning into a turf war and I stepped in and negotiated, first with Mickey."

"I explained to him how much money the Mob in New York and the Chicago Outfit were taking in. 15 million so far this year, and there's still five months left. I told Mickey, if he and the Dragna brothers kept fighting, this all would stop. I said none of you, not you, Mickey, and not the Dragnas would live to tell the tale."

"Esther, Mickey was a sourpuss, as usual. He still complained about losing his new suit, so Essie, I handed him 25 grand to tone down the damage, and offered to be his attorney with the insurance company. I assured him that he would make a large profit on the damage to his house and to his suit. All he had to do was stop fighting with the Dragna brothers, or else the boys from New York would step in and clean house. Mickey agreed and pocketed the twenty five grand."

Abe finished telling his story to Esther.

"I went across town to meet with the Dragna brothers. I sat them down to give them an education about the flow of cash to the Mob in New York and to the Chicago Outfit. I let them know that, if they were the cause of this war, they had best stop or they would be the losers."

"I threw out a fastball and told them I just put out fifty grand to Mickey to guarantee he would stay away from their territories. I let them know I wanted my money back, now!"

"The brothers squirmed but paid the money. My last word was if anybody had grievances they could come to me to settle their problems."

"So, Essie, I made 25 grand and laughed all the way to the hotel."

30

CHARACTER FLAWS & BLACK EYES

Abe was spending one week a month in Beverly Hills, coming home to Chicago to work at the office. Abe and Ralph were together a few times each week, supposedly doing union business in Cicero at one of Moses Annenberg's businesses. It was run by a notorious madam, Sheeny Rose. When the meetings were over, Abe would go home to the Drake, his suit perfectly pressed. Esther could see that it had been hanging in a closet.

She suspected Abe was in bed with another women. Although it hurt her to think about it, she knew that he had this character flaw. Ralph's coming around did not help. The friends reinforced each other's bad habits.

Abe always came home to Esther. He loved her and she loved him blindly. They had a good friendship and business partnership. She did not want to knock over the pushcart. Their eleven years together were only getting better because she looked the other way.

Esther and Hannah were on a day trip, seeing clients. Hannah mentioned, "Hey, we're very close to one of our clients."

"Really? Who would that be?"

Hannah, snapping her gum, answered, "Sheeny Rose, and she owes 175 dollars for last week's pony bets."

"Jesus, Hannah, I should have put you on commission! Are you saving this money or just having fun?"

"Esther, I'm giving the cash to our sisters, and even Alvin. Best yet, I'm telling them the money comes from both of us."

Esther ordered her driver, "Mike, take us to Sheeny Rose's."

Esther was curious about what this woman looked like and what the big attraction was for Abe.

Upon arriving, Esther and Hannah left the limo and walked to the elegant, old brick building. Esther wisely gave a shave and a haircut knock on the front door. It opened immediately.

Esther and Hannah were led into the parlor and greeted by Sheeny Rose, herself. Rose asked Hannah what she was doing there. Hannah retorted, "You missed collection last week and you owe me 175 dollars for the ponies--bad luck on Leaping Lena in the fifth. She threw the jockey around the first turn."

Rose looked at Esther. "Are you Hannah's bodyguard?"

Hannah quickly introduced her. "This is my boss and older sister, Esther Teitelbaum."

Rose, looking Esther up and down, said, "I'm told you're quite an accomplished attorney."

Esther got angry. "And I heard you're nothing but a two-bit whore!"

Hannah, ever cheerful, said, "I just knew you two would get along fabulously."

Rose stared at Esther. "I could fill you in on a thing or two about your husband and which girls he spends time with."

"I don't want to know what Abe is doing and I will rearrange your face if you don't stop talking."

"I'm sure you've noticed his suits are never wrinkled, and it's not because he irons them. Get my drift?"

Esther could not hold back any longer.

She grabbed Rose by the neck and threw three quick jabs to her face, then a roundhouse left hook to knock her flat to the ground.

"Hannah, it's time to go. I will cover the losses that Rose owes you."

As they walked out the front door, Rose yelled, "Get out and never come back!"

Esther snapped, "Does that include Abe?"

"I can't believe you actually hit me, you bitch! Now I know why Abe comes here so often."

Esther, now truly upset, started toward the bloodied Rose. Hannah pulled her back.

"She's not worth breaking a nail! Come on, Esther. Let's get out of here!"

Esther smirked at Rose, who was cowering and mumbling something about telling Moses. Esther grabbed her again and pulled her to her feet. She reminded Rose that she worked for Esther's client, and that was why she was allowed to stay in business.

Esther warned, "Never talk to me like that again or I will really hurt you."

Hannah was trying to lighten things up. "We've been thrown out of worse places, and by the way, you are cut off. I'm not taking your bets any more."

Esther was shaken. Although she'd fought many fights in the

ring, she never hated her opponents before. This was different.

When they got back to the apartment, she asked Hannah to fix her a sherry on the rocks.

Esther washed her hands and face. She picked up the phone, called the office, and asked Abe, "Have you received a call from Moses?"

"Moses hasn't called. What's going on?"

"Abe, I wanted to let you know we have been banned from Moses' house of ill repute."

"Why were you there to start with?"

"Curiosity almost killed the cat. Rose was talking ill about you and who you've had been sleeping with and I pasted her severely, left hook, I think. I know she learned a lesson about discretion."

Abe started his spiel: "Esther, whatever she said, it was all lies. I would never..."

Esther cut him off, her eyes nearly closed in anger, her voice more serious than Abe had ever heard before.

"I do not want to hear this nonsense! I knew who you were from the time you told me you had an unconsummated marriage. I have known about your flaws, but I chose to look the other way because we're best friends and a good team.

You are the only one I love. Do you understand me, Abe? No more!"

A very stunned Abe choked up, "Yes, Essie, I will try."

"Try, Abe? I'm not expecting miracles from you, but be forewarned, if I ever hear this kind of talk again I will make a call! Do you know what I mean?"

"Yes, Essie."

Esther slammed down the phone.

Abe called Moses Annenberg. "Moe, do we have a problem?"

"Yes, we do! Rose got a broken nose and two of the biggest black eyes I've ever seen. She can't work for a couple of weeks. Other than that, what problem?

"Also, Abe, if Esther wants to fight anyone I will book her fights and give odds. Nobody ever shut Rose up before. I told her if she gives me any more problems, I'll send Esther over to counsel her."

31

THE WISH LISTS

Between 1935 and 1940, during the times Abe was in California with Ben, Esther would spend time with her six younger sisters. She would take them to lunch and shopping for new clothes, and, for their birthdays, fulfill their wish lists.

The sisters liked to tell family stories. This is when they missed their older sister, Rosie, the most. Rosie would visit from San Francisco, but not often enough to be part of the ongoing lunch bunch.

While Abe was going to California with Ben, Esther was able to do the research. Often, she was able to settle the pending cases, before Abe went to court.

Her parents, Tillie and Herman, were happy. They drove across the country to visit Rose in San Francisco. They were gone for more than a month, coming home with many new stories of their adventures.

The sisters loved these new stories! They had heard all the old family stories, from 1826 to 1903, over and over: about brave great-grandmother Freda and how she got the family away from the pogroms and the danger in the Jewish Pale of Settlement in Russia and Poland.

The sisters talked about their lives and what they wished for. Hannah made a list of what could be given as gifts for birthdays. They would gather at Tillie's home for birthdays and holidays. Hannah imagined the reactions on their faces as they received their gifts.

Esther loved her sisters. She had parented all of them, except for Rose. Now her sisters were getting married. They were starting families, except for Nora, who didn't care about marriage, only about having fun.

Abe, too, had a wish list, and the top item was children. Esther was not ready. She rationalized not yet having children by telling herself that they were helping her family during the Great Depression with the money that they earned from their law practice.

An obstacle in their relationship was Abe's obsession with the almighty dollar. It worried Esther. Abe was gambling daily, armed with information he was getting from the Outfit's bookies. Moses Annenberg's wire was giving Abe tips.

It made Abe happy to play the ponies, bet on baseball, or wager on which way a bird would fly.

Esther couldn't complain. She and Abe were helping her family with needed funds and much more.

She believed that, should anything happen to her or Abe, her family would reciprocate the help that she and Abe had lovingly given to all.

32

HIDING IN PLAIN SIGHT

When Ben Siegel traveled to Chicago, he would visit the office, bringing presents for Esther and Hannah.

He told them stories about Hollywood stars. He talked about the attention he was receiving, and the work he was doing with the unions, including the problems between Mickey and the Dragna brothers. He made sure all of the operations were going smoothly. Ben planned to open The Screen Extras Guild, with other unions supporting the idea. (He was successful.)

With Abe's help and the Outfit's blessing, it was just like back in the time when members of the Mob left New York City (when the police and aggressive District Attorneys were breathing down their necks).

The guilty could run off to Hollywood and become movie extras, hiding in plain sight!

Every month, the Outfit would send people to join the new guild. They went to work, but certainly not for the standard six dollars per day. They had money and great wardrobes. The men had overcoats, hats, and even tuxedos. The women had fine dresses, jewelry, and fur coats.

When they were not working for the studios, they were working for Mickey Cohen as collectors, bookies, and even loan sharks.

Many of the women were dating the heads of the studios and giving valuable information to Ben, who was controlling the guilds and unions connected with the industry. It was almost like witness protection, only better: the mobster extras were not government witnesses.

33

OFFSPRING

In April of 1939, Esther called Abe in California to tell him she was pregnant. Before the end of December, they would have a baby. Abe was very excited and started making plans for the future.

They had been living at the Drake Apartments since they were first built in 1929. Abe wanted a proper home in which to raise a family. He started looking for a house to move into before the birth of their first child.

He purchased a home on Hawthorne Place in Chicago from a distraught client. The client sold it to Abe for far below market value and mysteriously left town in a hurry.

In May of 1940, the Teitelbaums moved into the great three-story home, furnished with everything anyone could want.

Esther hired cooks and housekeepers who kept the house spotless and always ready for friends and relatives to visit.

The music room, on the top floor, had a marble floor and great acoustics. The Chicago Symphony string section practiced there on Tuesdays and Wednesdays. Beautiful music echoed through this incredible home, which included an indoor swimming pool.

Abe and Esther were happy here. They felt safe and comfortable. They could continue working, knowing things were going to be perfect for the new prince of the family, little Albert. He would never want for anything.

34

BENEVOLENT ASSOCIATION

Tony Accardo took control of the Chicago Outfit and ruled with an iron fist for several decades.

Ralph Capone delivered documents from the federal prosecutor to the Teitelbaum office. They included indictments for fourteen top members of the Chicago Outfit, including for Alphonse, who was already in prison for charges related to unpaid taxes on beer.

The prosecutors were trying to put the rest of the Outfit in prison, threatening sentences of two to four years.

Esther had spent weeks on the research and knew she could confound any prosecutor. She prepared a writ that would throw the court system into turmoil.

To make the matter more interesting, the judge was an old

friend of the law firm. Esther told Abe that that he had an appointment with the judge in his private office.

Abe showed up Monday morning at the judge's office to present the writ that Esther had drawn up. The judge gave it to the federal prosecutor. After reading the paper, he looked at the judge and shook his head.

"We jumped too early. This writ will stand up in court. I recommend the court react before we lose the case."

The judge took back the writ. "Go back to your office. I will call you when and if you are needed."

When the federal prosecutor left the office, the judge told Abe, "The federal case has holes and I will quash all of the indictments immediately. We will not be bothering your clients."

On the way out, Abe placed an envelope containing fifty grand on the desk for the Benevolent Association. The case was dropped, never to be looked into again.

This proved that the Teitelbaums really could fix anything.

Business with the Outfit went on as usual.

Esther and Abe were the darlings of the Chicago Outfit.

35

PROMISES KEPT

Abe presented the writ and arguments (that Esther had worked on for years) to the Federal Court. All the hard work paid off on November 4, 1939.

Abe paid the federal fines under protest. He sent a telegram to the court stating that all fines and obligations in the matter of the United States versus Alphonse Capone had been paid.

He was able to get Alphonse transferred from Alcatraz to Terminal Island Prison, Long Beach, California, for the remaining seven months.

As promised, Alphonse was released, having served seven years and four months, not the twelve years to which he had been sentenced in 1932. Alphonse went home to Florida. He, too, hid in plain sight.

Alphonse Capone was never again in charge. He stayed out of the limelight. Every few years he and Ralph would visit his family and the Teitelbaums at their homes in Chicago. He succeeded in visiting old friends, family, and doctors, and then going back to Florida, without making any waves or meeting the stink eye of the newspapers.

36

NO TEARS FOR FRANK NITTI

When Alphonse Capone was sent to prison, his first cousin and henchman, Frank Nitti, who had served as Al's Sicilian connection, personal bodyguard, and murder agent for the old South Side Gang, became his successor. Nitti used Mob soldiers and others for the violent acts rather than do them himself. As he rose in the organization, Nitti's business instinct dictated that he must personally avoid doing the dirty work. That was what the hit men were paid for.

Frank had just spent eighteen months in prison. Being confined in a small space resulted in claustrophobia. He became paranoid about returning.

Frank ran the Outfit in a way that resulted in some members becoming very unhappy that he was chosen to be the boss.

What Frank didn't know was that Paul Ricca was really calling the shots.

The Outfit put up with Frank for about two years, and then he was put out to pasture. He never regained stature, nor had the ear of the Outfit again.

Legal issues surfaced again for Frank when the Feds charged him, along with Paul Ricca, Nick Circella, Charlie Gioe, and Phil D'Andrea, with putting pressure on the Hollywood studios. This created havoc in the movie industry by prompting strikes and violence in the unions.

The Outfit was not pleased. When Frank's lawyers told him that, if convicted, he would serve an even longer sentence, he decided to cheat the government out of their trial.

On March 19, 1943, Frank left his home, walked to the railroad tracks, and shot himself. His first shot missed the mark, blowing his hat off and grazing his head.

A second attempt succeeded. He ended his life, to the government's disappointment.

The Outfit's members did not shed any tears over Frank. Actually, they celebrated that he went off to the "Big Casino." The newspapers disrespectfully printed photos of Frank, at the railroad yard, on the front pages.

37

PASTRAMI FROM MA GORDON'S

Abe began spending more time with Ben in California. They stayed at the Beverly Hills Hotel in a large suite, close to exits so that people could come and go without being recognized.

Abe and Ben had many visitors, from union reps to midnight calls from the hiding escapees from Sheeny Rose's house of fallen and wayward girls. (The girls flocked to Hollywood to be in the movies and to date the studio chiefs.)

During one of these California trips, the suite was full of friends from Chicago. There was a knock on the door. Everyone was escorted into the master bedroom. Ben opened the bedroom door.

There was a delivery of kosher food from Ma Gordon's: pastrami and everything else that could be ordered, in true

Abe style. Abe laid it out on the dining room table and dug into the food. He made a huge plate, and then sat at the head of the table.

Ben opened the bedroom door. The boys from Chicago and the six girls that Big Judy (a confidante of Sheeny Rose) had sent over from the Guild, were getting acquainted. Ben picked up the phone and made another call to Big Judy to obtain fresh ingénues for himself and Abe.

The party was off to a great start! Booze, a piano, and a trio of musicians were rolled into the room.

Abe was enjoying his sandwich when Ben came in. "Put the freaking sandwich down. Big Judy sent over some pretty girls."

Abe, the food lover told Ben, "I can always get a girl, but a great pastrami sandwich from Ma Gordon's is too hard to pass up, especially with mustard and garlic dill pickles!"

Around two in the morning, another knock came at the door. It was Big Burt, an Outfit collector, sent to pick up a package. He took one look at the lively room and told Ben, "You guys sure know how to throw a party!" Burt asked why they were dressed up. Ben said they were going to Cantor's for a late-night snack.

Burt blurted out, "Abe sure can eat!"

Ben added, "He earns and he eats. What can I tell you? Money follows him around like a new puppy. I've always been proud to stand next to him."

Abe interrupted, "Burt, do you want go with us to Cantor's?" He was excited to let him know Cantor's had great streusels. Burt decided to go with Abe and Ben, and they ended up spending the entire weekend together.

When Burt left on Monday morning, Abe gave him two hundred grand in a large heavy briefcase.

Burt knew that the Outfit had a full year of union contracts, signed, sealed, and delivered, from all the studios and unions that Ben controlled.

38

WHO FARTED?

On the way back from the airport, Ben suggested that they pick up Mickey Cohen and see what trouble he was getting into. Ben directed Ronnie, the driver, to Brentwood.

They picked up Mickey, who was still grumbling about the Dragna brothers making more money from the unions. Abe and Ben smiled. Ben said, "Relax. We're all making more money than we can count."

Abe and Ben were sitting in the back seat of the limo and Mickey was sitting on the jump seat, looking directly at them, when Ben started fanning the air. All eyes immediately looked at a smiling Abe, who was patting his belly. Ben frowned.

"Oh my God, Abe, I told you not to pull this shit in my new

car!" Abe was smiling to himself as Ronnie rolled down all the windows. Ben was hanging out the back window, gagging, and Mickey was holding his hat over his face.

Ben pulled a gun on Abe. It was so absurd that they all started laughing. "Abe, I can't shoot you. You haven't changed since we were kids and you asked me to pull your finger, and that was over thirty years ago!"

Mickey put his hand out to Ben and said, "Pull my finger."

The laughter continued until Ben said to Mickey, "If you ever fart in my car I will shoot you," which started the laughter again.

All the windows (including the privacy window) were shut by Ronnie, and the boys talked business while being driven around Los Angeles and Santa Monica.

39

OPPORTUNITIES IN VEGAS

That evening, Ben told Abe over dinner, "Meyer asked me to go to Nevada with his old friend, Moe Sedway. He's been working for Meyer and together we're going see if there's an opportunity to set up business."

Meyer had political friends and judges in his pocket. Ben had decided to go to Las Vegas for Meyer to assess the plans for the New York Mob. Moe knew the owners of the El Cortez hotel and casino. Ben was looking forward to new opportunities.

Abe warned, "Ben, Nevada is a shit hole and the big money is always going to be in Hollywood and Los Angeles. The business is already established and there's no one we can trust in Nevada." Ben felt that, since Meyer asked this favor, he had to go, just to look around.

The next morning, Ben took Abe to the airport to go back to Chicago, and then drove to Las Vegas.

40

THREE YEARS OF VIOLENCE OVER

Abe arrived at Midway Airport and took a cab to the office, where he was greeted by Esther.

"Abe, you've been gone a long time. There's so much to catch up on, both business and work, starting with court tomorrow. You need to see this."

Esther handed Abe the newspaper. The heading was about the problems among the six service unions in Chicago.

Violence had broken out and things had gotten out of control over the last three months. Abe hadn't worked with the unions since 1935.

Within the week, Abe made deals, greasing the wheels with the workers and the unions and his own pockets.

All the problems ceased, ending three years of violence in Chicago. There was no need to send flowers. There were no more weeping widows or fatherless children.

41

A LITTLE MISUNDERSTANDING

Esther and Abe were working well together. Things were pretty good at home in Chicago.

That changed when Tony Accardo took over the Outfit after Alphonse was sent to prison and Frank Nitti shot himself.

Tony was upset with Abe for charging him a $125,000 per year retainer for legal services. Tony finally gave Abe a check. He asked him to hold it for a week, when he would have the cash dropped off at the office.

Eight weeks later, Esther came upon the check, still sitting on Abe's desk. She deposited it into their office account.

The bank reported the transaction to the IRS, which immediately questioned Tony about where the money came from.

Tony, a little upset, put out a $25,000 contract on Abe's head.

Ben Siegel got wind of it and called Abe, who was in Los Angeles. Ben arranged a sit-down with Tony, Murray Humphreys, Abe and Ben.

"Murray's reputation as 'The Smoother' was well known and respected. Abe has been the Outfit's fixer ever since he started working for Capone. He makes our problems go away and keeps most of the Outfit out of jail."

Murray asked Tony to stop the hit on Abe, reminding him to always pay in cash and to never have anything in writing, especially a check. His advice was respected and well received.

Tony acquiesced and told his thumpers to stand down.

Esther changed the books and turned the check into a loan, not a retainer, knowing there was not a tax position on loans. Following up with a letter to the IRS did the trick. They dropped the investigation.

Abe was a master at finding the squeaky wheel and applying the grease. He was known as "The Fixer" for the Chicago Outfit.

Tony and Abe continued doing business together, in cash, for many years.

42

SWIMMING WITH SHARKS

Things were going smoothly in Chicago. Abe again was traveling to California to meet Ben. Abe kept trying to persuade Ben to not get involved in Nevada. Ben wanted to develop a new home for the Mob in the West.

In 1943, Ben had arranged for the purchase of some land in Las Vegas. He was spending money on business plans that were never to his satisfaction. Meyer and Lucky were funding the project from their petty cash.

Abe realized that Ben was not only hooked on this deal, but also hooked on Virginia Hill, his close companion.

Virginia was a party girl who dated many Mob members from New York, including Joseph Epstein, Frank Costello, Frank

Nitti, Joe Adonis, and Tony Accardo from Chicago, before hooking up with Ben.

As long as Ben was controlling Mickey Cohen and the Dragna brothers, the Outfit and the Mob were not complaining. The cash was flowing.

Ben's friend, Abe, was always able to advise him in a safe direction when swimming with sharks.

Back at the office, Abe received a call from an excited Ben.

"Meyer wants to break ground on his project by 1945. Meyer and Lucky are advancing me 1.5 million dollars."

"Come to Chicago, Ben, and help me understand what you promised to Meyer and Lucky, and how the deal is to be structured."

Ben agreed and flew into Midway the next week. Abe picked him up at the airport. Ben immediately started talking about his Vegas deal.

"I purchased a great piece of land that will be the center of elegance and power for me and the boys. Everything was going smooth, except I spent a little too much on the plans and the purchase. I'm still not happy with the plans, exactly, and had them changed three or four times. So far, the only cloud is that I'm now over budget, without a shovelful of dirt to show for my hard work."

Abe said, "Take a breath. Did you spend all the cash Meyer and Sal advanced for the deal? Don't tell me you spent all of it plus 500 grand of your own money?"

"Ben, you spent a lot of money on this shit hole and now you should cut your losses and make arrangements to pay back Meyer and Salvatore before it becomes terminal. I suggest you get back to the real money machine in California. Don't you realize we are bringing in over $15 million a year now? We're making good money. Why are you fucking around in Vegas?"

Ben was not ready to give it up. He always had to finish whatever he started, even when he found himself in deadly trouble.

Abe was scratching his head and getting a headache. "What will this project cost, and when will it be finished?"

"I won't lie to you, Abe. The cost will be a little over five million. I believe it can be finished by December, 1946. Virginia Hill is helping as coordinator for the project."

Abe was shocked at how reckless this deal was and reminded Ben, "This deal is over your head and you do not write your own deals. The money comes from a tight fist in one hand and a gun in the other."

"Now it's getting risky and possibly deadly."

Ben smiled. "Abe, who would shoot me? Don't worry, Abe, everybody thinks this is my deal, so it's me on the hook, not you or Esther."

Ben and Abe went their separate ways. Ben went back to his deal, and, Abe, to his practice.

43

DEBRIEFING

Abe and Esther were very busy, but not too busy to have more children. Abe was practicing his art of debriefing. He dreamed of having a big family.

Albert had arrived in December of 1939. Celeste was born in January of 1942, Anne on July 4th, 1943. Now there were three. More children were planned.

Abe was very happy with his children and invited the relatives to gather at their home on Hawthorne Place.

On occasion, clients would visit for dinners and meetings. Ralph Capone would come over to drive Abe to meetings or gambling and even to Sheeny Rose's whorehouse. Esther still turned a blind eye.

Another child, Robert John (that would be me) was born on

September 22, 1945. I was welcomed into the family with open arms.

Ralph told the good news to Alphonse in Florida. Ralph planned to pick him up and take him to Chicago to see Al's doctors.

Al had a set of child-sized cufflinks made for the new baby. They were exact replicas of .38 revolvers, with mother-of-pearl handles and revolving cylinders, made out of 14 karat gold by his jeweler in Florida.

Three weeks later, Ralph brought Al to Chicago to visit his doctors, but first they went to see Esther and Abe and their new baby. They stayed for dinner. Alphonse and Ralph gave Esther the cufflinks for little Robert.

Esther secreted the gift in the bottom of a music box for five years before allowing Robert wear them at a dinner party. Robert was smartly dressed in a French cuff shirt and a camel hair jacket. After the party, Esther put the cufflinks safely away for many years.

44

MAHONEY'S LAMENT

Abe was in court defending two young thugs who happened to be friends of Esther's mama, Tillie.

Abe had two cases that day and had all the information he needed from Esther's research to get the second case, for manslaughter, let off. This would look good for the Outfit.

This morning, he had breakfast with the judge who wanted Mahoney in prison. Abe did not mention that Esther had found a legal precedent that he could use to get Mahoney off. They finished eating and left to court separately.

Abe appeared for the Goodman brothers. "Your Honor, may I please approach the bench?" The judge asked Abe to approach. Abe spoke softly to the judge. "The two boys have done some very bad things, but I see that you have bigger fish to fry today in the City of Chicago versus Mahoney. I would be happy to have Mahoney plead guilty, so that you could just slap the wrists of the Goodman brothers and set them free."

Abe walked back to the defendant table and sat down next to the brothers. The judge picked up his gavel and pounded it twice.

"Will the defendants please rise? After reviewing this case, I find lack of evidence to continue this action." He pounded the gavel again. "Case dismissed! Prisoners are released."

The District Attorney started to object but was eyed by the judge and remained seated. He did not want the wrath of this judge to come down upon him.

Abe went to the holding cell at the courthouse. Mahoney was escorted into the room and shackled to his chair.

Abe told him, "If we go to court today and plead innocent, the judge will throw the book at you. You'll wind up in prison until you are an old man, 25 years or more at best, for 2nd degree manslaughter."

"My advice is to throw yourself upon the mercy of the court by pleading guilty."

Charles was shaken but said he would listen to Abe.

HIDING IN PLAIN SIGHT

In court, the bailiff called out, "City of Chicago versus Mahoney, step forward and be heard."

Abe winked at the judge and said, "Your Honor, my client wishes to change his plea."

The judge asked, "Charles Mahoney, do you understand what this does to your case? Have you come to this of your own accord?"

Mahoney answered, "Yes, sir, Your Honor, and I am truly sorry for my actions."

The judge delivered his decision. "Charles Mahoney, you shall be remanded to state prison at Joliet to serve ten years at hard labor for second degree manslaughter."

He pounded his gavel and instructed the bailiff to take Mr. Mahoney away.

Back at the office Abe was greeted by Esther with, "How did it go in court today?"

"I ate breakfast with the judge and it was made clear that he was going to throw the book at Mahoney, so, after discussing the alternatives with the judge, I got Mahoney to change his plea to guilty. He got ten years in Joliet."

Esther was unhappy with this. She had done some serious research, knowing Abe could get him off scot-free. That would have been a feather in his cap, in the eyes of the Outfit.

Abe said, "The good news is I got the Goodman brothers off with a wrist slap."

"That's nice." Esther reminded Abe, "Their parents are friends with Tillie."

Abe laughed. "Tillie is good friends with half our clients."

Esther laughed, as well. "Abe, let's stop on the way home and get some good food."

Abe grinned. "That's better than your mama's cooking, that's for sure."

45

NEVER TELL THAT ONE

Esther smiled. "Since we're going to Mama's tonight for dinner, we could visit my old room and play hide the kosher 48." Both Esther and Abe were grinning like Cheshire cats.

Abe asked, "Could I tell some limericks that I learned in my youth?"

Esther was laughing. "As long it's not the one about a man named Dave."

Abe shared a new one, hoping to impress Esther.

> *A limerick can be furtive and mean,*
> *If not controlled, can become obscene.*
> *When it gets down to verse.*
> *And really perverse,*

It's best to keep it clean!

"Now that was nice Abe, a real charmer."

Abe continued, "There once was a lady from Dallas who used a dynamite stick as a…"

"No, Abe, please don't tell that one to anyone, ever."

"Okay, Essie."

That night, the children were with the governess, maids, and other household staff, a bodyguard, and Nicky, a new guard dog. Nicky was always upstairs, protective of little Robert and the other three children.

Abe and Esther said good night to the children, gave instructions to the staff, left their home, and entered the awaiting limo. They instructed their driver to go to Mama's.

They soon arrived on Clark Street. The whole family greeted Esther and Abe, including sister Rose. Dinner was served and Abe was surprised that it was not burnt. It had been perfectly cooked, not by Mama, but by Rose!

What a night it was, with all the stories and all the food they could eat!

At the end of the evening, Esther took Abe by the hand and led him upstairs to her old bedroom. She was surprised that it was exactly the way she had left it. They made good use of the room.

Abe said, grinning ear to ear, "That is the girl I remember!"

Abe had given Hannah a handful of fifty-dollar bills and told her to give them to her sisters, as a gift from him and from Esther.

She performed this distraction well. Abe and Esther were upstairs, playing hide and seek in the bedroom to which Abe used to sneak, twenty years earlier, when they were in law school.

Esther packed some of her old memorabilia in a suitcase. She walked downstairs to an awaiting flock of sisters.

Time went by. Abe and Esther were living a full life, with children and all the work they could handle. Family and friends filled their home frequently.

Esther found that she was never alone--not even for a day.

46

MUSIC & HEAT

Abe had to travel occasionally, but not like he did in earlier years. Esther was happy to have him around. He loved the children and gave them every material thing a child could want, although not much of his time.

He was always preoccupied with work, gambling, or planning for relatives to visit for extended stays.

Upon returning from a business trip to New York, Abe found several of his friends visiting in the conference room of his office. They acted like kids at old home week.

The friends were Ben Siegel and Mickey Cohen (visiting from California), Ralph Capone, Louis Romano, Sidney Korshak, and Allen Smiley.

When the business talk was over, they would play the ponies and Hannah would take care of the book. They played craps or cards and when the trade got rough they pitched coins for fun.

Hannah, who always beat Ben in pitching quarters, was getting coffee when Ben asked if anyone would like to up the stakes and pitch silver dollars. A unanimous "yes" sounded including from Hannah. Ben smiled and took a hundred dollars cash from each player (except Hannah) and he put in two crisp one hundred dollar bills.

Ben sent the bodyguards to the bank to get $700 in silver dollars. When they returned, the friends began pitching the silver dollars against the far wall.

Mickey was the first to grumble when Hannah, the last to pitch, tossed a leaner on the wall and picked up all the coins.

Within an hour, Mickey Cohen was cleaned out of all his money. "I'm not so sure about this. Losing all this cash while pitching against a woman? Something is dreadfully wrong here!"

"You, Mickey Cohen, are just a sore loser! Since you are so upset--and believe me, I don't do this often--I'll give you a chance to win your money back, double or nothing, on the next pitch."

"I'm in, but I'm pitching first!"

Mickey, took a dollar and pitched it. It hit the wall and rolled away one inch. Mickey was delighted.

Hannah turned her back to the wall. Looking over her shoulder, she looked Mickey right in the eye and said, "Music and heat, a buck down and a buck a week."

She lofted her dollar into the air. It hit the top of Mickey's dollar and leaned against the wall, to the cheers of all the boys except Mickey. He walked to the table and sat in a chair, the wind blown out of his sails.

He pulled out two hundred-dollar bills and handed them to Hannah. He shook her hand, sneering.

Everyone was still cheering. It took Hannah only an hour to clean all out of their silver dollars.

Allen Smiley asked Ben, "Does she ever lose?"

"Not since I've known her!"

Abe and Esther entered the conference room and found Hannah struggling with the heavy bag of 700 silver dollars. Mickey, still prune-faced, said, "Esther, I wish you and Abe came into the room a lot earlier, before Hannah kicked our asses."

Esther laughed at Mickey's misery. "Next time, Mickey, know your odds. I taught Hannah how to pitch coins when she was a little girl and sometimes she even beats me! Would you like to pitch coins with me, double or nothing?"

Mickey grumbled, "No, I would not."

47

SIDNEY'S EDUCATION

In Super Mob, author Gus Russo relates that, during the 1955 Las Vegas union strikes, Sidney Korshak could not close the deal. After six weeks of construction strikes at the Riviera Hotel, Sidney called Abe Teitelbaum for help. Abe said he would do the job for $50,000. Sidney agreed. Within the hour, Abe made phone calls to men he knew on both sides, from when he worked for the unions in Chicago.

Abe had a lot of friends. He always said, "It's good to have friends on both sides of an argument."

Each side gained what it wanted and the strike was over.

Abe collected cash payments from both sides!

Sidney picked up the phone to Abe. "Isn't $50,000 a lot of money for a few phone calls? Can I get a break on the price?"

Abe said, "Look, Sidney, it took me forty years to learn how to do that. Would you like the picket lines to go back up?" Sid sent the cash to Abe Teitelbaum that same day.

Early in 1943, Sidney and Abe entered Esther's office to talk about Murray "The Camel" Humphrey educating Sidney about the sweetheart deals with the unions.

Abe explained, "Murray was Capone's fixer and started the ball rolling with the dry-cleaning establishments, creating the phrase money laundering. Now, I do all the union work, so listen carefully!"

This was the beginning of Abe's mentoring of Sidney Korshak.

"I always felt that I was doing what good lawyers do: first protect our clients, then hire people to create space between our clients, the unions, and management."

"That way, nothing could be traced back to the Outfit. It was with very specific instructions to funnel corporate monies to the Outfit in exchange for labor peace."

"Sid, it's that simple. We spread around a lot of money to the unions and management reps, $3000 or $5000. We're just buying off squeaky wheels to make arrangements with dishonest union and corporate officials."

Abe continued, "You know, Louie Romano and I control six

different service unions here in Chicago, and there are no strikes unless I make the phone call."

Sidney, a good student, recapped what he needed to do: "I make cash payoffs to the business agents, then collect from both the employers and the workers. This way we'll keep the peace with the union and the studios in California."

Abe stated again, "Sid, you'll do great. Just use my modus operandi and funnel the exact piece back to the Outfit. I want my envelope every month, and, remember, if you have trouble, call me."

"Those problems will quickly go away or flowers will be sent."

48

CALIFORNIA

A few days later, Abe sprung a surprise on Esther.

Confused and angry, Esther said, "Abe, I do not like the idea of the children and I moving to Palm Springs! We have plenty of security. This would uproot most of my family."

"Essie, I will keep our home here. It would make me feel better to know that you and the children were out of harm's way."

"Listen to me, Abe. It's not our children or me that's in danger. It's you who could not keep a low profile. Those gangsters are trying to shoot you or throw you out a window."

"The children and I are safe, and I'm needed here in Chicago to do our research and to keep our clients out of jail."

Esther dropped a bombshell.

"Abe, I know that you've been seeing Roxanne. She's a friend of my sister, Norma."

"And speaking of Norma, I know you've been with her, too! Can you deny you gave her money?"

"Damn it, Abe! They're only eighteen years old! I will not overlook this like I did when you and Ralph went to see that whore Rose. She's not a threat to our children or me. I know you're just playing there and letting off steam."

"Stop or I will take care of you, personally!"

"You better start worrying who I'll tell about this, like Harry Bernstein, or even your uncle Harry. They would not look kindly at what you're doing. They'd be more dangerous than the occasional thug that takes a pot shot at you."

"Essie, please calm yourself. We have dinner plans with the Capones. Let's talk about this tomorrow night."

"Okay, but I have put you on record that I will not put up with your wandering with my family or their young friends. Do not ever shame me in front of my family again!"

A few weeks later, Abe convinced Esther to take a trip to Palm Springs to see how beautiful it is.

Without telling her, he had already purchased a ten-bedroom house with a large pool in the heart of Palm Springs.

It was a quaint city with good schools. Many Hollywood stars had second homes there.

The Mob made sure that everyone was safe against any threats. Deals could be made safely in Palm Springs between the Mob families of Chicago and New York.

Esther reluctantly agreed to accommodate Abe, with the stipulation that he move her entire law library to Palm Springs, so she could do her work.

Abe reassured Esther that her relatives would visit often because many of them had already moved to the West Coast.

He promised he would be there every weekend, which she knew he would not do.

The house was beautiful--everything Abe had promised.

After eight months of family visits, however, they found it was not big enough to host all their guests.

Also, they needed a more private location where clients could do business or hide out.

Abe's well-known friend, Allen Smiley, was already living there.

(I suppose Allen earned his small town persona because he lived in the Coachella Valley before it became Palm Springs, a destination for Hollywood stars and snowbirds).

49

LOVELESS RANCH

Abe Teitelbaum's friend and client, Walter Kirschner, had built the Tower Ranch in La Quinta, where Franklin Delano Roosevelt and General Patton stayed during World War Two. Kirschner was always building new estates. (He was a powerful developer, owning many department stores in Los Angeles and Chicago.)

Walter was a great friend and political supporter of FDR, traveling with him to every stop on the presidential campaign trail.

When Walter suggested that Roosevelt move to Palm Springs, FDR told Walter that that was not his preference, as it was not private enough.

Kirschner then built an estate on his ranch in Indio, only

twenty miles from Palm Springs. It was a magnificent house on ten acres. It had a three-acre compound surrounded by eleven-foot high walls, with another tall wooden wall, for extra privacy. There was a five-room Secret Service house, parking for forty cars, three enclosed garages, plus quarters for the live-in maids, butler, and driver.

The kitchen had four double-door refrigerators and four six-burner stoves, with grills. This kitchen could feed one hundred people!

The estate had gardens, tennis courts, and an Olympic size swimming pool.

Had President Roosevelt not died in office, the house would have been his.

After Roosevelt's passing, Walter visited Abe in Palm Springs. He knew that Abe was looking for a bigger and safer place for his family. Walter asked Abe to drive to Indio to see the Loveless Ranch.

Eleanor Roosevelt despised the heat of the Coachella Valley, saying, "It's too damn hot!" She left to return to Val-Kill in Hyde Park, New York.

Walter needed a new buyer for the project. He and Abe drove into the secure compound and Abe was immediately delighted. He walked the property, then promptly wrote a check to Walter Kirschner for $127,000.

Walter drove Abe back to Palm Springs and made calls to his office. Within a week, Walter delivered the deed of sale for this functional and charming property.

Abe called his older sister and younger brother, making a deal for them to purchase the Palm Springs property.

Abe moved Esther and the children to the Loveless Ranch, the most beautiful and secure property in the Coachella Valley, fit for a President of the United States of America.

50

DEMISE OF ALPHONSE

Abe was working with a client at the office when he was interrupted by a call from Ralph.

"What's going on, Ralph? Oh no! Where? I'm leaving now. Yes, I'm on my way to Midway to catch a flight."

Abe cut short his meeting, telling the client that he was needed in Florida, and abruptly left.

Upon arriving at the Alphonse's home in Miami Beach, he was met by Ralph.

"Abe, we're glad you're here to keep the press away so we can bury Alphonse with dignity."

"I never expected Snorky to go so quickly. I am truly sorry,

Ralph. I will do everything in my power to help your family, as always."

"Abe, you and Esther have been our family's protectors for the last twenty years. I never said this to you, but Alphonse and I always talked about how you looked like our brother, and, to tell the truth, you have always acted as if you were."

Abe placed a hand on Ralph's shoulder as they walked into the living room. The family was gathered around the radio, listening to the news.

News flash! Today, January Twenty-Fifth, Nineteen Forty Seven, Alphonse Capone passed away quietly at age forty-eight. He will be remembered in a private, simple funeral service, reminiscent of the cloistered last years of his life.

Attorney Abraham Teitelbaum revealed that the once-rich Alphonse Capone died penniless.

The palatial twenty-five room, Palm Island estate where he died was heavily mortgaged.

The next day, Abe took a plane back to Chicago. He had court appearances and depositions to deal with in the Windy City.

Abe was met at Midway Airport and driven to the office. He immediately called Esther at the Loveless Ranch.

"Essie, how are you doing? Great. How's the baby? Good. I'm

coming back to the ranch next week. Yes, I will stay for two full weeks. I'm just finishing up some court work. Okay, kiss the children for me."

"Come home, Abe. The children need you and I miss you. How is Alphonse's family doing?"

"Essie, the whole family is broken up. You can call them if you want. Have you finished the files I sent you?"

"I'll call Ralph today and talk to the family. Abe, all is ready for court, and you know it hit the papers."

"Essie, it's still dangerous here for you. The thing in the papers was a close one, just thugs wanting to take my position with the union. Lucky for me the police had their office bugged. They gave me police protection, plus the names: Needle Nose Labriola and Jimmy Weinberg. I gave this information to our friends and we will not be bothered by them again."

"You're pushing your luck, Abe. On top of everything that's going on, Bernstein has been calling, saying that you have some woman living there with you, in our house."

"Come on, Essie, that's my sister, Ilana, and some of my brother's children. That Bernstein is like a rat spreading rumors like lice."

"I want us to spend more time together. There are concerns

we must address. Damn you, Abe! Some things I don't want to know! Things are dangerous. I want you to close up our office and sell our home. It's time for you to move to Beverly Hills."

"Don't be silly, Essie. Chicago is where we make our money. I can't kill the goose that lays the golden eggs. I'll be home soon. Ben and Allen will come and visit."

"Nice ducking, Abe. How is Ben doing? I see in the papers that the casino and hotel in Las Vegas opened and closed in December. Do we have any exposure there with Meyer or Salvatore?"

"Esther, there is no exposure. I never liked that deal and I stayed out of it. What I have done is advise him, as a client and friend, to never get in too deep. Ben will be staying with us for a few days, and we'll spend some time catching up. What's most important is that you and I will be together."

"Ben is not bringing that little big mouth Mickey Cohen with him, is he? I'm embarrassed to say I still want to hit him in that prune face of his."

"No, Mickey is not coming. He's busy being the big shot for the little shit that he is. Just Ben and Allen Smiley will be down. They're looking forward to spending time with us and catching up with our family."

"Sounds like old home week. I'm very sorry for the Capone

family. Alphonse was always a gentleman to me, even though he did a lot of terrible things. I'm very sad he died this way, I know this has taken a toll on you."

"You are right, it has. I'll see you soon. Kiss all the children for me and give them my love. Good bye, Essie."

51

BIG CASINO

Ben arrived at the Loveless Ranch. Esther ran up and hugged him.

"Ben, it's so good to see you! I'm happy that you're going to spend a few days with us. We'll catch up and have a little fun in the sun."

"Great to see you, Esther! I needed a break and I needed to spend it with Abe and be normal. I want to see your kids and lay by the pool, get some sun and relax. May I stay in the pool house?"

"Of course. Also, Hannah is here with us. I bet she can still kick your ass tossing coins! She's taking care of the children by the tennis courts."

"It will be good to see Hannah. Abe told me she married the

bodyguard. You make me feel like I'm safe at home. Thank you, Esther. Abe and I need to talk about business. Now please excuse us."

Ben and Abe walked through the rose garden to the pool house and sat next to the pool.

"Ben, that loudmouth Harry Bernstein showed up to visit Esther. He confronted me about having Roxanne at my home in Chicago, and even threatened me to stay on the straight and narrow with Esther or he would cause me trouble."

"Abe, don't worry about him. He also showed up in Beverly Hills last week. Then I called Meyer. He told me that Harry was a rat with a big mouth."

"I can assure you that Harry won't be seeing you or Esther again. The last time I saw him he had lead poisoning three times. He hit the Big Casino."

"Thanks for the good news."

"Abe, good news often comes with bad news. About the Vegas deal... the opening of The Flamingo was a disaster, a major fuck up, with a big rainstorm and no one showing up. I had to close the casino. The reopening was not good but it's getting better. It'll take a year or so to pay back the money. It's costing a lot more than I expected. Abe, I need two million dollars soon or Meyer and Salvatore might punch my ticket."

"Look Ben, I don't need to know where the money went. How much do you really owe Sal and Meyer, and how can I help?"

"Abe, I owe the boys six million. I'm selling some stock in The Flamingo, including some of my shares. Can you spot me $500 grand until the deal is worked out?"

"It'll take me a week to get my hands on the cash. I'll have to go to Chicago for it. Please don't tell Esther about Bernstein. She'll think I took out the mortgage on his farm. The truth is, I'm glad he hit the Big Casino."

"Abe, I just took out that rat bastard like the garbage he was, just as a favor to Meyer. I'm glad it helped you."

"Ben, I'm going to make arrangements to go to Chicago."

"Thanks, Abe. Now I just want to lay in the sun. Virginia and I had a bad fight a year ago. She left and stashed away two million from my casino funds in a Swiss bank, right under my fucking nose. Now she sees the light. I'm in big trouble. She gave the money back to me. We're now getting along and the money will help with the pay back."

"She took that money? She's lucky you didn't punch her ticket. Virginia must be great in the sack, like a breath of fresh air. Sorry. Enough of this! I'm not trying to stir the pot. Ben, the phone is in the pool house by the fireplace. It's a private line."

Ben went to the pool house and made a call.

"Allen, I'm at Abe's ranch. Can you pick up Virginia and bring her here for a few days? Yes, I talked to her. She'll be ready by noon. Thanks. See you this afternoon."

A new black Buick with Allen Smiley and Virginia Hill arrived through the double gates and entered the compound. Carlos Martin, Abe's California bodyguard, met them.

"Allen, how are you doing, sir? Just park over by the wall please."

"Nice to see you again, Carlos. This is Virginia Hill. She will be staying with Ben for a few days."

"I'll take her luggage to the pool house. Just proceed past the green gate and into the house. Ben is with Abe, Esther, and the children, having dinner."

"Thanks, Carlos. By the way, what's your fighting weight?"

"One hundred fifty pounds. Why?"

"Same weight as Mickey Cohen. He also was a class boxer. Did you know he lost a featherweight title fight in 1931?"

"Esther told me she could beat the shit out of Mickey. Now it's 1947 and I'm in my prime. I know Mickey. Do you want to back me and win some cash?"

"We'll see. Congratulations on marrying Hannah. She's a great woman and a friend from Chicago."

"Thank you, Allen. If you need anything let me know. I can get you anything you need."

Virginia walked into the main house and gasped. "Wow this is great! Fit for a king!"

"No, Virginia, for a President!" Abe said.

"This home was built by Walter Kirschner for Franklin D. Roosevelt. That's why there's so much security."

Ben stood to greet Allen and Virginia.

"Virginia, this is Esther and the family."

Esther shepherded the new arrivals to the table. "Come on, let's all sit down and have dinner."

The dining room table was large enough for twenty people. The adults were sitting on one end, and the children, controlled by Hannah and two governesses, were seated at the other. The staff served a lavish dinner.

Esther raised her glass to make a toast.

"To my family and our friends from Chicago and Beverly Hills. After dinner, Virginia, I will give you the tour of our home."

"Esther, I would like that."

After dinner, Abe, Ben, and Allen excused themselves and walked to the pool house.

Ben opened the conversation. "Things are getting complicated. I just talked to Meyer. He wants me back in Las Vegas. I told him it would be a few days because I have things to take care of."

"I'm sorry to hear this. Esther wanted to spend some time with you. When are you leaving?"

"Tomorrow. Abe, I'm giving most of my shares of The Flamingo back to the boys, along with the two million that Virginia took. Now, with the $500,000 from you, I can deal myself out of this mess. I'm walking away with only 10% of the casino. I did build my dream and it will grow. Ten per cent of paradise is better than nothing."

"Ben, are you broke?"

"No, Smiley, I'm not broke. Hollywood is still like a printing press for money. I'm just sorry that I didn't control this deal close to the vest."

"I'll take you home tomorrow."

"Thanks, Allen, I'll be staying at Virginia's house. Abe, we better go tell Essie. She will be disappointed."

The next morning, Ben Siegel, Virginia Hill, Allen Smiley, and Abe and Esther Teitelbaum gathered at the main gate, which was being opened by the bodyguard.

"Sorry, Esther, that we could not stay longer, but business called."

"Always wonderful to see our dear friends. Ben, we must get together again soon. Virginia, it was nice to meet you. Allen, drive carefully."

Ben hugged Esther and Abe, then got into the waiting car, driven by Allen.

Abe said to Esther, "I don't like this. We could have talked to Meyer for Ben."

"Sure, Abe, but who could talk to Salvatore without jeopardizing us?"

"Good point, Essie. I'll keep my mouth shut."

The Teitelbaums walked back to the interior of the compound and watched the children play in the pool with Hannah and a governess.

52

TOSSED LIKE USED KLEENEX

On the evening of June 20, 1947, Ben Siegel sat on the couch in Virginia's bright, beautiful living room. The front door opened and in walked Virginia Hill, her brother, Charles, and Allen Smiley. They had just returned from a day at Santa Monica Beach. Virginia and Charles went upstairs. Allen sat down next to Ben.

"The beach was great tonight. You should have come with us. We ate at the same place we were last night."

"Yes, Allen, I know, but I needed some time alone to work out a deal with Meyer. I offered him half my preferred stock plus the two and a half million of the six million I borrowed. Now all I owe is a measly three and a half million. I think they will be satisfied. After all, it's only business."

"What did he say?"

"Meyer said everything would work out for the best. It was what he did not say that causes me to wonder. I'm not going to worry about this. I should have stayed with Esther and Al for a few more days, floating in the pool, working on my suntan."

Ben picked up a newspaper. "Allen, look at this on page two, about the studios."

At that moment, nine shots were fired through the front window. Five hit Ben, two in his head, ripping out his eye. One bullet burned the coat of Smiley, who dropped to the floor, absolutely quiet. A high power car could be heard tearing away toward Sunset Boulevard.

Allen heard screaming from upstairs, and the wails of sirens as the police cars arrived.

The Beverly Hills police questioned Allen in the kitchen while Dr. Hansen attended to him.

"You really are lucky. That bullet just grazed your forearm. You're just bruised. Use this ice. Here are a couple of pills to settle your nerves."

"Thanks, Doctor. I'm very shook up. Ben was my best friend. I still can't believe this. We were just talking and then he's dead."

Detective Miller said sternly, "Smiley, please talk to me, not to the doctor. I'm the detective here. Since you were sitting next to Benjamin Siegel when he was shot and killed, I must detain you as a material witness. Get your things. We're going to the department as soon as we're finished."

"If I'm not under arrest, may I use the phone to call my lawyers?"

"Sure. We have some time before we'll be done here. You don't need to go into the living room. We're preparing to photograph Ben's body, so just use this phone in the kitchen."

"Operator, I need a person-to-person call to Abe Teitelbaum, Indio California number 7-3-4-8-4. My name is Allen Smiley. Thank you."

The phone rang at the Loveless Ranch. Esther and Abe were in bed. Abe reached for the phone.

"Hello. Yes, this is Abe Teitelbaum. Sure, yes, I will take the call."

"What is it Allen? It's 11:30! What's going on? You're being held as a material witness? Tell me exactly what happened. Ben? No, this can't be true! Yes, Esther and I will be up tomorrow. We'll stay at the Beverly Hills Hotel."

Abe hung up the phone, in shock. He told Esther. They comforted each other on the loss of their lifelong friend.

The next morning, the bodyguard drove Esther and Abe to Beverly Hills.

"Abe, I feel so sorry. Ben was just with us."

"Ben knew the rules and he broke them. He told me that if he didn't take risks, he wouldn't reap the rewards. I advised him many times to stay out of Las Vegas. I got a call early this morning saying that, last night, The Flamingo was taken over by Moe Sedway and Gus Greenbaum. They're working for Meyer and moved in just an hour after Ben was murdered. The casino is doing business. Meyer and Lucky tossed Ben out like used Kleenex."

In their room at the Beverly Hills Hotel, Abe and Esther were talking over breakfast.

"Esther, is Dr. Maurice Siegel, Tillie's doctor, here in Beverly Hills?"

"Yes, why? Ben introduced Mama to him, and you met him at Mama's house on Edinburg."

"No one is allowed at the funeral, not even us. Maurice and the rabbi are interring Ben at noon. This is not right. We were his best friends."

"Abe, we'll go later this afternoon, when it'll be private. I know the place. It's Beth Olam in Hollywood. Abe, please call the driver to bring the car around. I don't want to sit here any more. Let's visit Allen over on Sunset. Let's be with our friends."

Later that afternoon, when Abe cleaned out Ben's safety deposit box, he found an envelope with instructions to give it to his ex-wife and children in New York.

There was also a handwritten note from Ben to him. Abe read the note and wept. He felt remorse that he was not able to protect his friend. He folded the note and kept it with him, tucked in his wallet, for the rest of his life.

Abe, with a full suitcase, went to the front desk of the hotel and spoke with Bernice, his favorite clerk.

"I want to thank you for all you have done while Ben and I stayed here. This is for you, for keeping it all quiet."

Abe handed Bernice an envelope with five thousand-dollar bills.

"Oh, Mr. Brown, it was never a problem, and you are always welcome here."

"Please book my suite for Mr. and Mrs. Abe Teitelbaum and four children starting the last week in June through the first week in September, for the next few years, as it's too damn hot in the Coachella Valley!"

Bernice looked confused and asked, "Where is that place?"

"Palm Springs. It's very hot in the summer."

Bernice still looked confused and held up the envelope. "Is this a deposit?"

Abe smiled and said, "No, this is from Ben and me to you, for your help and understanding these last few years."

He left the lobby and joined Esther in the waiting limo.

53

A HORSE AT SARATOGA

On November 20, 1947, at the Teitelbaums' law offices in Chicago, Abe received research from Esther. She was in California, going through court cases for early December.

His secretary, Shirley, informed him, "Abe, Allen Smiley is on the phone."

"Hello, how are you? How's California?"

"I've been working with Mickey and things are smooth. Abe, can you do me a big favor?"

"Sure, anything. Allen, what do you need?"

"I have a horse at Saratoga I want to bet. I don't want anybody to know that I'm betting on this race. I want a grand on his nose. Will you do this for me?"

"Ok, I'll do this for you. I want to bet on this nag, too. Is that all right with you?"

"Abe, bet on whatever you want. All I want is a grand on Whiff-and-Poo's nose in the 4th race today."

"I'll get us down. I'll call you later with the results."

Abe called his Chicago bookie. "Louie, I want two grand on Whiff-and-Poo to win in the 4th at Saratoga."

"Look, Abe, I have to lay this off. It may take me a while. I'll call you back."

Abe started calling his list of bookies. He made his third bet with the same results: "I gotta lay off the bet and we'll get back to you."

Abe always said if he was in for a penny he was in for a dollar.

An hour before the race went off, calls came in to Abe's office. When it was all over, Abe Teitelbaum had 20 bets down for $2000 each on Whiff-and-Poo's nose.

"Abe, you have a call from Moses Annenberg."

Abe picked up the phone. "Moses, how are you doing?"

"Abe, I hear you're onto something big so I have my wire next to the phone. You can listen to the results in two minutes."

"Great, Moses, thank you."

Abe listened on the phone, stood up, and jumped on top of his desk, screaming, "I won! I won! I won!"

Abe had $39,000 on the horse. He had just won $331,500. Smiley had $1000 that paid him $8500, which made him very happy. A very ecstatic, lucky man yelled to Shirley, "Call Esther!"

"Okay, Abe. She's is on the phone."

"Essie, we have the luck! I hit the big one! We must contact Louie Romano in Long Beach. We're all going on a trip around the country to collect a lot of cash."

"Sure, Abe, this sounds great. Hannah wants to stay with our sister Rose for a month in San Francisco. The timing couldn't be a better. I can get a couple of my sisters to watch the children at the ranch and we can spend much-needed time together."

"We'll leave the middle of January and go for a couple of months."

"Nineteen-forty-eight, Essie, is going to be our best year ever!"

54

COLLECTIONS

January 15, 1948. Abe and Esther made plans with Louis Romano to go on a two-month trip around the country.

They would travel by train, first class, to see clients and to collect Abe's winnings from the bookies.

Esther asked Hannah, "Have you told Chane and Norma everything they need to do while we're out of town?"

"Essie, don't worry. I wrote everything down, including phone numbers. I will be at Rose's home in San Francisco. Our sisters have your office phone number. They can call and locate you anywhere during the next two months. I gave them the locations by date."

Chane added, "Esther, go have some fun. We have everything. The kids will always be cared for. They will want for nothing. I'm happy that I have my little Roger and all the children here with me."

Norma said, "Get into the car and don't worry! I'll watch over Chane."

"Thanks, Norma. Bye!"

The limousine drove through the gates as the family waved goodbye.

The train pulled out of Union Station. Louis and Esther were talking while Abe slept. "Esther, I'm so sorry about Ben. I haven't talked about this in the last six months. He was hotheaded but I really liked him."

"Yes, Ben was like a brother. I'm not in the trenches like you and Ben were. I only do the research to get everyone set free, but this senseless killing gave me a real wake-up call."

"The epitaph that Meyer put on Ben's headstone saying 'From The Family' was detestable."

"Esther, I know this is how we make our living. Sometimes, what we're doing makes it worth it. I never liked carrying a gun. It just made me a big target."

"Louis, people always said that you were not a cowboy, just a very serious man. Truth is, someday we all must pay the piper."

Abe woke up. "Your Honor, that is my summation and I'm sticking to it! Hi Esther, hi Louis! I was just napping."

"Of course you were, Abe. You nap a lot. What were you dreaming about, my friend?"

"About a client that was being charged in court for murder. He stated the man was dead when he arrived."

"Ok, Abe. Enough. We know this one." Esther had heard it hundreds of times.

The Teitelbaums spent lots of time on the train. They met with bookmakers around the country, collecting money that was owed to them. Esther placed it in the hatbox. She never let it out of her sight.

When in big cities, they stayed in grand hotels, ate in the finest restaurants, and spent time with friends.

55

DEATH OF INNOCENCE

On March 18, 1948, toward the end of the collection trip, Esther and Abe were getting ready to check out of their suite at the Grand Hotel in Miami. The train to California was to leave at noon. Louie was next door, packing.

There was a knock at the door.

Esther asked, "Who is it?"

"Telegram for Esther Teitelbaum."

Esther opened the door. "Thank you."

"What is it, Essie?"

"It's a telegram from Dr. Paulie, Abe. We must get back home as soon as possible! All the children are sick with the bird flu, and Linda has pneumonia."

Esther, Abe, and Louie traveled by train from Florida back to California. It took two days.

On the morning of March 20, 1948, the Teitelbaums were met at the station by the bodyguard, accompanied by Dr. Paulie.

"Abe, Esther, I am so sorry. Linda passed away around midnight. There was nothing anyone could do. I am so sorry," Dr. Paulie said, in a near whisper.

Esther fell to her knees. Her broken heart allowed a scream--a primal cry to the heavens. Abe reached down to lift her up. Her knees were bleeding from the rough sidewalk.

"We must get back to the ranch, Esther. There are things to do."

Dr. Paulie offered a sedative to calm Esther. The three hour drive back to the desert ranch was punctuated by anguished cries and quiet sobbing.

My father and the bodyguard heard nothing, as the window between the front and back seat was raised, sealing out Esther's sobs.

Dr. Paulie did his best to comfort Esther, but he was a poor substitute for an absent husband. Esther broke down.

Funeral arrangements for Linda were made, and she was laid

to rest at Beth Olam in Hollywood, only 50 feet away from the Teitelbaums' friend, Benjamin Siegel.

56

CONFUSION

The Teitelbaums' children did not attend Linda's funeral. They were all sick with the bird flu that had claimed their sister.

For the next ten years (1948 to 1958), Esther continued as best she could, putting on a brave face.

She rarely came out of her room. When she emerged, dressed up and smiling, it was to host parties for civic leaders and elected officials, including Governor Knight and senators. There were parties for the children's birthdays, Brownies, Girl Scouts, Cub and Boy Scouts, and for the PTA and Women's Club. When the Mob and Outfit members would visit to talk business, Esther would stay in her room. She didn't want to see their faces ever again.

Abe and Esther separated, but remained law partners.

Although Abe had a new family in Chicago, he continued to visit Esther and his children at the Loveless Ranch.

For many years, Esther continued to do all of Abe's research, sheltering him from federal indictments and criminal charges.

Eventually, Abe moved his second family from Chicago to Beverly Hills.

From 1949 to 1958, Abe cheated on his second "wife," Roxanne, (they were not married) by sleeping with Esther during his visits to the Loveless Ranch. He then went back to Beverly Hills and cheated on Esther with Roxanne.

57

LIKE SANTA ANITA

It was June of 1953. Abe was talking with Esther at the Loveless Ranch.

"I cannot stop what the papers print. They are crucifying me in the news, Esther. I'm sorry for trying to improve the Indio fairgrounds with a 400-acre gift of a racetrack, just like Santa Anita,"

"Now they printed that I am a Mob front with bad influence in the Valley."

"Yes, Abe. You're very high profile."

"These shmucks don't realize that a racetrack here will bring the city millions."

"I told them my partners would gift the property to the city.

Then they would own the buildings and the track with no cost to the city, not a thin dime. All I wanted was to manage and control the gambling."

"My investors would put up all the money. The City of Indio is turning down a huge deal and getting nothing."

"Yes Abe, the city must be brainless because they don't want mobsters living here, handling their money. You can see that your friends are not welcome."

"I just don't understand. They took my $40,000 for a public swimming pool and never put our name on it, those ungrateful putzes!"

"Just give it up. You won't win this one."

The bodyguard walked into the living room.

"Sorry, Boss, but you need to see the newspaper."

"Let me see. Damn! It's on the front page! Esther, listen to this: 'Senator McClellan proposed a permanent national crime commission, with subpoena power, to expose the gangster infiltration of the Chicago restaurant industry.'"

"Carlos, get the car. I need to get to Los Angeles!"

"Abe, please listen. I still have political friends. I'll ask them to lighten up on the printing of the news where we live, for the children's sake."

"Esther, I know. Please do whatever you can to stop the papers. Right now I have bigger fish to fry, and this one stinks."

"Robert Kennedy and McClellan are working together. If they want to play, I will denounce Kennedy's father, Joe. He has a lot to hide and I know it first hand."

58

DISMISSAL

1953. Abe was having lunch with Allen Smiley at Nate & Al's Restaurant.

"Albert is going to be thirteen and he needs to study this summer for his Bar Mitzvah. Can he stay with you so he can go to the school on Beverly?"

"Sure, Abe that's no problem. What's going on in tax court?"

"Esther wrote a beautiful reply to the court and they are so confused, they took my case off the docket. Esther said that, with their three best investigators, it'd take five years just to get their heads out of their ass. Then she'll file a motion for dismissal."

"That's great. How is Esther doing? I haven't seen her since Linda died."

"Esther is busy doing research for me. She's on Governor Knight's task force on drugs and she throws parties for kids' birthdays or for local politicians. When she's alone she still cries all the time."

"When do you see your kids? "I spend two weeks at the ranch in January and two more in July. That's when I see my children.

Our friends come in from New York and Chicago so they can talk freely behind those high walls. The rest of the time I'm here in Beverly Hills with my other kids and Roxanne. She drinks like a fish, then causes me trouble. Last week, she stabbed me with a goddam fish fork. I thought Ben had women trouble!"

"Abe, I'm still upset about Ben. I wish he never went to Las Vegas."

"I miss him too, Allen. He liked to play with that snake, Virginia, and then he got bit. Ben just would not listen to good counsel. Allen, it's your turn to pick up the check. I must be going."

59

FIFTH AMENDMENT

July 10, 1958. Senate investigators were concerned about the rumor of the alleged 1954 plot to kill the lawyer of the family of Alphonse Capone, Abe Teitelbaum. Abe was on the list of witnesses set to testify before the committee.

Teitelbaum was a central figure in the 1951 tax scandals. He was placed on probation after being convicted of income tax evasion.

Three weeks later, at the Loveless Ranch, the family was listening to the news on the radio. Abe Teitelbaum and Louis Romano were called to testify, along with many others from the Chicago Outfit. Most, like Abe and Louis, pled the Fifth Amendment.

"I respectfully decline to answer on the grounds that it may incriminate me."

After the committee session ended, Robert Kennedy, the committee counsel, told the reporters that it was the notoriety surrounding Teitelbaum's tax difficulties that led to the conspiracy to kill him.

Robert Kennedy cornered Abe in the hallway.

"Teitelbaum, I'm completely amazed that, after your conviction, the courts felt compassion for you and did not disbar you. This is beyond me, and now you're still hiding behind the Fifth Amendment."

"Yes, I use the Fifth Amendment to protect the people from a rat like you. Ergo, you are correct, you little pompous prick, still hiding behind your father's coattails."

"This is just a friendly reminder that your father, Joseph, caused more damage than Alphonse Capone did, even in his best years, so stop the bullshit! If you persist in putting me on the stand I will talk about your father's past, in detail."

After this encounter with Bobby Kennedy, Abe Teitelbaum was never again called to appear in front of the Senate Racket Committee.

60

UNCLE BEN HAS FAMILY

1969. Esther was dressed up as if she were going to court. She was having breakfast with her uncle, Ben Melnick, who was penniless and reading a racing form.

In 1928, the Outfit had blackballed Ben on the orders of Al Capone. No one would help Ben again. His fall from grace was absolute.

In 1956, Ben had been reduced to selling penny insurance for the Chicago Sun Times all around the Midwest. He stayed at his niece Chane's home in Glencoe, Illinois.

There was just so much business and the money was lean. Ben traveled around until he landed in California in 1966.

Again feeling a sense of family obligation, Esther took him in, giving him a home until he passed away. He was family.

"Esther, thank you for all you have done for me. I know that I was not a good uncle. I caused you lots of trouble over the years. When I had nowhere else to go, you never hesitated for a second. I am eternally grateful to you for what you have done."

"Ben, please don't mention this again. What you did back in 1928 doesn't count any more. Let's never talk about this again. I will make sure you are comfortable for the rest of your life."

"Thanks, Esther, can you give me twenty bucks? I have a hot one in the sixth race at Santa Anita today and we'll split my winnings."

"Of course, Ben. How are you going to get to the track?"

"There's a bus for ten bucks from the Farmers Market to the track." Esther handed Ben fifty dollars.

Esther's driver from the law firm knocked on her door. "Good morning Esther are you ready to go to work?"

"Yes, Henry, let's go. I have a lot of fires to put out today."

Upon arriving home, Esther was greeted by Uncle Ben Melnick, who handed her an envelope containing three hundred dollars. She put it into her purse and said, "Thank you."

Uncle Ben had always gambled, but this time, and for the rest of his life, he was fortunate with the long shots!

61

ABE TEITELBAUM 1906 - 1980

Abe "Pop" Teitelbaum, after being released from prison, spent six days a week at at my store, Los Angeles Coin Exchange. He invited his old "friends" to have lunch and share memories, and was running up my tab at Art's deli.

Not much had changed. My father never found his way out of the limelight. He was still chasing the almighty dollar.

He enjoyed running around with old friends from Chicago. He was living rent free in Beverly Hills (an extended stay at the Ramada Inn, which was owned by one of his grateful clients).

He was still collecting "favors."

Like Pop always said, "It is good to have friends in high places that owe you favors."

When he died in 1980 at age 74, his funeral played out like his life: full of chaos and drama.

The families gathered. The crowd included my mother and siblings, plus Pop's second family of my half brothers and sisters, and Pop's sister, our aunt.

The tension between my mother and aunt was just as strong as it was in 1932. When we got to the Chapel at Mount Sinai for the service, a third family from New York met us!

They were wailing big crocodile tears. They got up to greet us, introducing themselves as our brothers and sisters from New York City.

There were six supposed siblings, new to us, older, all with spouses!

We listened to stories about Pop visiting them during the last couple of years, which we knew were not true.

I stood up and announced that the estate of our father was insolvent, that any cash he received since he got out of prison came from me and from my half brother.

My brother and I had kept track of Pop's whereabouts at all times. We funded him so that he would have self-respect, not empty pockets.

Our normally prim Aunt Pauline shocked the crowd by

saying something so improper that people blushed: "You say you're a Teitelbaum? Drop your pants and I will be able to tell if you are a Teitelbaum or not."

My mother, Esther, turned away and laughed till she cried. She finally let go of the hate she had felt for her sister-in-law all those years. She reached out to shake her hand. "Nice job, Pauline."

Pauline looked quite smug as the third "family" left. They did not go to the gravesite. It's tough to con a con!

We never heard from them again. They were in it for the nonexistent money, only. I'm confident that they had a long and costly flight for nothing.

At the gravesite, we were still somber until our half brother, Kim, screamed, "I can't live without my Pop!" and tried to jump into Pop's open grave. (Pop had supported him most of his life, so his statement might not have been far from the truth.) Kim's drama caused the mood to lighten up. (Kim died two years ago, we all stood at the gravesite recalling this story).

Later that day we all told stories about Pop.

Our father, Abraham Teitelbaum, kept secrets from both of our separate families.

The Melnick side of the family, including my siblings, nieces, and nephews, went to the Beverly Wilshire Hotel to continue the storytelling and to spend time together.

My young nephews were on the balcony, inexplicably throwing food down to the street.

One of my siblings, who will remain nameless, went into the restroom to smoke a joint. Each sibling was called to the restroom to partake (separately, so our mother would get not get suspicious).

Eventually, she had to go to the restroom. She got high from all the smoke in the small room.

When she emerged, I couldn't help but blurt out the guilty sibling's name!

Mom was feeling no pain, and told stories we had never heard before. She'd finally let go.

She laughed as she recounted what Pauline said at the funeral. "I always knew that our family was strange."

(For years, every time we saw Pauline, she would ask, "How is Esther? Is she still alive?" She considered her goal of outliving Esther to be a competition. Pauline won. She lived to be more than one hundred. When she died, she was surrounded by the Teitelbaum family on her brother Morris' side. They loved her very much.)

Between the pot-smoking and the food fight, the hotel room was a mess. We were charged extra.

It was worth it.

62

FALL FROM GRACE

My mother and father always made sure our family looked good. Esther was a classy woman, well dressed, intelligent, and strong. At any time in her adult life, when someone showed up for dinner, they would find the table perfectly set. It was important to her that things were done correctly.

My mother did the legal research and what she wanted most was to present a flawless case that would win in court. The client was not as important to her as her research and reputation.

My mother found good in the worst of her clients. Her mother had befriended many of the clients' mothers. Esther found that they had many things in common. This helped her to have compassion for them as sons, husbands, and fathers.

She felt her clients were harassed, treated unethically, and discriminated against because they were immigrants. She fought like hell for them.

My mother saw that law enforcement was just as crooked as the mobsters were when she was in law school in the 1920s.

After my father moved my mother and our family to Indio, California, Esther wanted to gain the respect she had earned in Chicago. That would not be easy in such a small town. The town was already gossiping about her: a story appeared in the local paper saying that she was Al Capone's sister.

Her best thinking brought her to Governor Knight's narcotics commission in 1951. She wrote a paper about the drug problems in the Coachella Valley and about the territoriality among cities. Each city wanted to be an independent entity, without sharing resources. She wanted to help the young people and the community to be free from drugs and gangs.

(This paper was read at a recovery conference in the 90s. When the audience was asked when they thought paper had been written, the consensus was "last week." When they found out it was written in 1951, they were shocked that not much had changed.)

Esther had grand parties at our ranch, with local and state politicians. There were dinner parties and fundraisers, sometimes with mobsters in attendance, although no one knew who they were.

The local residents came to swim, eat, and enjoy the wealthy lifestyle.

In the early 50s, stories appeared in the paper about Abe's building a public swimming pool and plans to build a racetrack.

No one knew the money for the racetrack would be coming from the Chicago Outfit, which would be in charge of the gambling. The property would be deeded to the city of Indio.

Abe and Esther were the darlings of the Coachella Valley and of Chicago.

Everything went according to plan until things went bad. A story appeared in the local paper about Abe's IRS problems and his ties to the Chicago Outfit.

After he stopped sending money to his family, Esther lost her standing in the community and had to leave town. She was already weakened by the death of her youngest daughter, Linda, who died of the bird flu in 1949.

She and her two youngest children moved to Beverly Hills to live with her mother, Tillie, and father, Herman.

Esther had always taken care of her mother's children. Now, ironically, Tillie was taking care of Esther's.

It was quite a shock for the children to go from being the richest family in town, living on a three acre compound, and a ten-acre ranch, to living with their grandparents in a two bedroom apartment.

The two school-age children were enrolled in the most prestigious schools in Beverly Hills. For years, neither felt like they fit in.

The illusion of Esther's perfect exterior had crumbled. It took until 1964, when she returned to work as an attorney, to gain back her confidence and again earn the respect she so desired.

Esther's daughter-in-law, Carol, was expecting her first baby and not wanting to lose her position as a legal secretary, asked Esther if she would fill in for her. Even though she knew Esther was an accomplished attorney, she felt it would do her much good to get back to work.

After only a month at the law firm, the attorney realized he could not keep her to himself. Esther was licensed to practice in California, Illinois, and the Supreme Court of the United States. He just couldn't have her doing secretarial work.

He called his friends at a prestigious law firm in West Los Angeles. They hired her immediately.

She mentored attorneys and taught them to win cases through impeccable research.

Esther worked into her late 80s.

She was honored at the Four Seasons Hotel in Beverly Hills, escorted by three members of the Secret Service (also graduates of John Marshall Law School), and by me, her son, Robert.

This reunion was one of her proudest moments and I was pleased to be able to share it with my mother.

After all the pain we shared, it was wonderful to have something to celebrate together.

Esther passed away a few months before her 90th birthday. She is buried in a mausoleum, down the hall and around the corner from her daughter, Linda, and her dear friend, Benjamin Siegel.

THE END

ACKNOWLEDGMENTS

Special thanks to:

HELENA SUTTON

DR. ROGER PASSMAN

DR. CINDY L. CARTER

DAVE PELZER

JERRY MOE, M.A.

JOHN BRADSHAW

JOHN LEE

DR. CLAUDIA BLACK

DAVID WHYTE

BRUCE FESSIER

STEPHEN M. LOPEZ, ESQ.

TIM BERTRAND

SEAMUS MCDONNELL

NORMAN FOX

The rest of this story

can be found in my first book:

Frogs and Snails and Mobster Tales:

Growing Up In Al Capone's Shadow

Website:

frogsandsnailsandMobstertales.com

ABOUT THE AUTHOR

Carol A. Teitelbaum

Carol has been a psychotherapist since 1985, with California private practices in Tarzana and Rancho Mirage. Her practice is dedicated to people who have experienced trauma, abuse, and addiction.

Bringing light into the darkness, Carol, along with her husband, Robert, created a 501 C3 corporation, Creative Change Conferences. This conference is celebrating its tenth year of offering help to survivors of child abuse. Her program, "It Happens to Boys," has helped thousands of men begin their healing process.

Carol is an author for Step 12 Magazine, Recovery Illustrated, Sober World, and Recovery View. She speaks at conferences and leads workshops.

Carol's conferences have included such stellar speakers as Jerry Moe, John Bradshaw, John Lee, Claudia Black, David Whyte, Dave Pelzer, Patrick Carnes, Rev. Leo Booth, many of whom Carol now calls friends.

Carol and Robert have been married fifty-four years have two children and three granddaughters, who are the loves of their lives.

Robert J. Teitelbaum

Robert is a SAG actor and retired casting director with twenty-five years in the entertainment industry. He has been the creative director of Palm Springs TheatreSports, an international improvisational organization, since 1994. He is CEO of Creative Change Conferences.

Robert speaks at conferences and leads workshops on Mob history, family dysfunction, trauma, abuse, addiction, and recovery.

Robert's first book, *Frogs and Snails and Mobster Tales: Growing Up in Al Capone's Shadow,* has helped many survivors find their voice.

Married fifty-four years to Carol, together they have enjoyed many adventures: having children and grandchildren, and being members of the huge family of Teitelbaums and Melnicks. Family and friends are what is most important to Robert.

He learned from his parents the importance of having people in your life you can count on.

FREEDOM OF INFORMATION ACT (FOIA)

Following are images of documents obtained from the United States Federal Government through the Freedom of Information Act.

FREEDOM OF INFORMATION ACT (FOIA)

ATTENTION

The following documents appearing in FBI files have been reviewed under the provisions of The Freedom of Information Act (FOIA) (Title 5, United States Code, Section 552); Privacy Act of 1974 (PA) (Title 5, United States Code, Section 552a); and/or Litigation.

☐ FOIA/PA ☐ Litigation ☐ Executive Order Applied

Requester:
Subject:
Computer or Case Identification Number:
Title of Case: _____ Section _____
* File
Serials Reviewed:

Release Location: *File _____ Section _____

This file section has been scanned into the FOIPA Document Processing System (FDPS) prior to National Security Classification review. Please see the documents located in the FDPS for current classification action, if warranted. Direct inquires about the FDPS to RIDS Service Request Unit, 202-324-3773.

File Number: **62-HQ-87960** Section **1**
Serial(s) Reviewed: **all**

FOIPA Requester:
FOIPA Subject:
FOIPA Computer Number: **999907**

File Number: _____ Section _____
Serial(s) Reviewed:

FOIPA Requester:
FOIPA Subject:
FOIPA Computer Number:

File Number: _____ Section _____
Serial(s) Reviewed:

FOIPA Requester:
FOIPA Subject:
FOIPA Computer Number:

THIS FORM IS TO BE MAINTAINED AS THE TOP SERIAL OF THE FILE, BUT NOT SERIALIZED.

ALL INFORMATION CONTAINED
HEREIN IS UNCLASSIFIED
DATE 09-27-2004 BY AUC 60290 PCK/AG/CLS

ATTENTION 999907

DO NOT REMOVE FROM FILE

FREEDOM OF INFORMATION ACT (FOIA)

☐ The enclosed material is from the main investigative file(s) in which the subject(s) of your request was the focus of the investigation. Our search located additional references, in files relating to other individuals, or matters, which may or may not be about your subject(s). Our experience has shown, when ident, references usually contain information similar to the information processed in the main file(s). Because of our significant backlog, we have given priority to processing only the main investigative file(s). If you want the references, you must submit a separate request for them in writing, and they will be reviewed at a later date, as time and resources permit.

☐ See additional information which follows.

Sincerely yours,

David M. Hardy
Section Chief
Record/Information
 Dissemination Section
Records Management Division

Enclosure(s) (2)

The Attorney General

Later in 1948, it was reported that Teitelbaum lived four miles west of Indio, California, in a home that was purchased for $125,000 cash. Data received concerning his bank transactions reflects that Teitelbaum has banked with the La Salle National Bank in Chicago, and reportedly had done some business with the Bank of America, Indio, California. In July, 1947, it is reported Teitelbaum made a request to the County Board of Supervisors, Riverside County, California, to build a 2½ million dollar race track in Indio, California.

It was also indicated that a Riverside, California newspaper checked the background of Teitelbaum and developed that he was a Chicago attorney, who had represented the Capone family for some years. It was stated he became interested in the affairs of Al Capone after the latter had been sentenced on an income tax violation in 1932. It is further indicated he represented Theresa Capone, mother of Al Capone, and that in 1942 he requested Al Capone's release from a Federal penitentiary on a habeas corpus writ. It is indicated he represented Ralph Capone and others when a $30,000 settlement was made of a Government claim of $119,367 on unpaid beer taxes.

In connection with the proposed race track, Teitelbaum was reported to have told a newspaperman, "I am a big man in this state, the State Legislature will have to prepare a special enabling act to make the track possible, but that can be handled. I can swing it with the legislature." He intimated that a small group of lobbyists and politicians controlled the State Legislature and those persons would be in favor of the race track.

Teitelbaum was apparently highly respected until the publication relative to the proposed race track, at which time it was made public that he represented the gangsters' element at Chicago. He apparently made large donations thereafter to the American Legion, Red Cross and civic groups, endeavoring to buy back good will.

In July, 1948, Teitelbaum allegedly resided in a rented residence at 850 North Kings Road, Los Angeles. It was also indicated that in Chicago, Teitelbaum was one of the attorneys used most frequently by the Chicago Syndicate.

Further information reflects that one Abraham Teitelbaum was active during 1947 and 1948.

b7C

DIRECTOR, FBI   June 21, 1948

RE: ABRAHAM TEITELBAUM

"The members, after the hearing, were removed to New York where they stood trial and were sent to the penitentiary for a $1,000,000.00 movie industry extortion.

"These included four hoodlums whose recent paroles have caused a lot of smoke in Chicago and Washington: LOUIS CAMPAGNA, PHIL D'ANDREA, CHARLES "CHERRY NOSE" GIOE, AND PAUL "THE WAITER" RICCA.

"After AL's death in 1947 TEITELBAUM announced that the once rich gangster died without will or property. Those on the inside track laughed at the announcement and said that AL's money had long ago been transferred to other names.

"His recent newsworthy ventures include the purchase of a Chicago Loop hotel building for $131000.00 and the purchase of half of the auditorium building, that graceful old Michigan Avenue landmark."

During an interview with Subject by a reporter for the Riverside Daily Press, TEITELBAUM made the following remarks: "I am a big man in this State", "The State Legislature will have to pass a special enabling act to make this track possible, but that can be handled", "I can swing it without the legislature".

The newspaper reporter further advised that at the time of the interview Subject had with him a copy of Dun and Bradstreet report to prove that he was a wealthy man.

The Bureau and the Chicago Field Division are requested to forward to San Diego any information they may have on their files that can be identified with Subject and the Bureau is also requested to submit a criminal record if one can be identified without a description or number.

94-29
HPH:dk
cc: File 39-20

cc: Chicago

ALL INFORMATION CONTAINED
HEREIN IS UNCLASSIFIED
DATE 09-27-2004 BY AUC 60290 BCE/AG/CLO

SAC, San Diego   July 12, 1948

Director, FBI

ABRAHAM TEITELBAUM
MISCELLANEOUS
INFORMATION CONCERNING
Your File 4-29

RECORDED - 76
EX-46

Reurlet June 21, 1948, requesting an identification record and background information concerning the captioned individual.

It has not been possible on the basis of the information furnished by you to locate a record for Abraham Teitelbaum in the files of the Identification Division of the Bureau. However, the Bureau's files reflect considerable information concerning one Al Teitelbaum, also known as Abraham Teitelbaum, who has been actively engaged in assisting the defense of Aaron Sapshoff, with alias, Allen Smiley, notorious West Coast racketeer, who is presently under indictment on charges of falsely Claiming Citizenship and Perjury. This individual is probably identical with the subject of your inquiry and it is noted in the same connection that the pertinent information concerning this individual is in the possession of the Los Angeles Division which, upon the receipt of this communication, should make such information available to you.

It is also requested that the Los Angeles Division furnish to the Bureau additional descriptive information concerning this individual in order that such information may be further searched through the indices of the Identification Division in an effort to locate a record for Teitelbaum.

cc - Los Angeles

ALL INFORMATION CONTAINED
HEREIN IS UNCLASSIFIED
DATE 09-27-2004 BY AUC 60293 BCH/AG/CLO
999907

BEST COPY AVAILABLE

FREEDOM OF INFORMATION ACT (FOIA)

Office Memorandum · UNITED STATES GOVERNMENT

TO : Director, FBI   DATE: July 30, 1948

FROM : SAC, Los Angeles

SUBJECT: ABRAHAM TEITELBAUM
MISCELLANEOUS
INFORMATION CONCERNING

Rebulet to San Diego dated July 12, 1948, carbon copy to Los Angeles.

The Chicago Office has advised that ABRAHAM TEITELBAUM, a Chicago attorney, has offices at 77 West Washington Street, Chicago, telephone number Randolph 1929. Chicago files reflect TEITELBAUM as for many years being on friendly terms with the CAPONE family and he has represented members of the CAPONE group in litigation. He has long been mentioned by reliable informants of the Chicago Office as being one of the leading attorneys for the Chicago underworld Syndicate. He is also reported to be in charge of the Syndicate's real estate operations in Chicago Loop property.

In September, 1946, TEITELBAUM was in contact with ALPHONSE CAPONE, former head of the CAPONE mob, and he also was in contact with ▮▮▮▮ b7C ▮▮▮▮ ALPHONSE CAPONE. It appeared that TEITELBAUM was handling the naturalization litigation concerning ▮▮▮▮ TEITELBAUM also was reported to be handling the contemplated divorce proceedings ▮▮▮▮ ▮▮▮▮ ALPHONSE, and he also was handling some unknown personal matter for RALPH CAPONE and requested the Mercer, Wisconsin, telephone number of RALPH CAPONE from the CAPONE family. He has purchased several properties in Chicago for large sums of money; however, the Chicago Office advised it is not known exactly which members of the Criminal Syndicate TEITELBAUM is fronting for at the present time and it is not known whose money is backing TEITELBAUM in his California ventures.

The Chicago Office reported it is said on best authority that members of the Criminal Syndicate "don't move without his authority."

TEITELBAUM is married and his wife's name is ESTHER. They have two children and now are renting a fairly large residence at 850 North Kings Road, Los Angeles. Information has been received indicating that they intend to remain at this address for approximately five months and will spend the winter at Palm Springs, California.

The Los Angeles Office has no information indicating a criminal record for TEITELBAUM. Also there is no information in our files concerning the date

RECORDED - 50
INDEXED - 50
11 AUG 3 1948

ALL INFORMATION CONTAINED
HEREIN IS UNCLASSIFIED
DATE 09-27-2004 BY AUC 60290 BCE/AG/CLO

Director, FBI   July 30, 1948

Re: ABRAHAM TEITELBAUM
    MISCELLANEOUS
    INFORMATION CONCERNING

and place of TEITELBAUM's birth, although he appears to be approximately 45 to 50 years of age. He weighs approximately 180 to 185 pounds, is about 5' 8" tall. The top of his head is bald and the fringe of hair is brown. His eyes are brown and his complexion is dark. He is of heavy build and might be described as fat. He speaks with an accent.

If the Bureau should be able to locate an arrest record on TEITELBAUM, it is requested that a copy be forwarded to this Los Angeles Office.

During recent months informants of this Office have advised that ABRAHAM TEITELBAUM has been closely associated with _____ with alias _____ who is presently under indictment in Federal Court on three counts of falsely claiming citizenship and one count of perjury. He has also associated closely with _____

b7C   _____ and TEITELBAUM have actively assisted _____ in connection with his defense, both in making contacts for him and in furnishing advice.

It is requested that the San Diego Office furnish the Los Angeles Office with information of possible value concerning the activities of TEITELBAUM in its Division.

LJL:PJG
39-95
cc: San Diego (44-29)

The Attorney General

About the middle of May, 1948, and prior to disposition of the [ ] prosecution, Al Teitelbaum, described as a Chicago attorney, together with [ ]. After the visit, information was received that Teitelbaum and [ ] discussed the case pending against [ ]. It was alleged that Teitelbaum attempted to assure [ ] that he would, or already had, taken care of the prosecution, [ ] Teitelbaum felt that arrangements could be made to have the Government drop the charges. It was further reported that Teitelbaum and [ ] considered attempting to make contact with U. S. District Judges J. F. T. O'Connor and Paul J. McCormick of the Southern District of California.

(39-2258-121)

On November 1, 1949, Acting United States Attorney Ernest A. Tobin, Los Angeles, advised a representative of this Bureau, that [ ] had approached the former United States Attorney James M. Carter, several months previous, in an effort to have the prosecution [ ] dismissed. Mr. Tobin said that he did not talk to [ ] and there were no witnesses to the conversation between Carter and [ ]

b7C

(39-2258-310)

On the basis of data available, a check of the records of the Identification Division of this Bureau does not reflect any arrest record for Teitelbaum.

Our Chicago Division informs that Teitelbaum is generally known as Abraham Teitelbaum, but occasionally is referred to as Al Teitelbaum. The current Chicago telephone directory lists him as Abraham Teitelbaum, 20 East Jackson Boulevard.

Information set forth above relating to the reported (39-2258-121) [ ] case has been furnished previously to the [ ] Liaison Section, informs that he received a telephonic request for a name check from [ ] of General Services Administration on Abraham Teitelbaum, and in addition on [ ] and [ ] who also testified before the King Subcommittee. References are still being checked on [ ] and [ ] will not furnish any information to GSA without specific clearance.

* Source was a technical surveillance.

b7C

cc: Mr. Ladd
Mr. Rosen
Mr. Winterrowd
Mr. W. F. Woods (Rm. 7649)
Mr. Martin
Mr. Hughes

The Attorney General   December 6, 1951

Director, FBI   PERSONAL AND CONFIDENTIAL

ABRAHAM TEITELBAUM, also known as,
Al Teitelbaum

The files of this Bureau contain information concerning one Abraham Teitelbaum, which may be of interest to you, and who may be identical with the individual by the same name, who recently testified before the House Subcommittee engaged in probing tax scandals.

In 1939, information was received by our Chicago Division, from [redacted] indicating that Abraham Teitelbaum, attorney with offices at 77 W. Washington Street, Chicago, Illinois, wanted to purchase material, including 10,000 adding machines and 10,000 typewriters, for the Mexican government. An investigation was conducted under the Foreign Agents Registration Act, which at that time required that such agents be registered with the Secretary of State. Teitelbaum, when interviewed, denied [redacted] story. He said he had a client, [redacted] who had been in Mexico for some time, and who was securing secondhand refrigerating units for importation into Mexico. Teitelbaum suggested that [redacted] was the individual supplying the refrigerating units as [redacted] Teitelbaum denied that he endeavored to purchase any material for the Mexican government.

[redacted] when later interviewed, said he probably had been mistaken and had misunderstood Teitelbaum's instructions. The United States Attorney's Office at Chicago, closed the investigation without prosecution, stating that no violation of a Federal law was indicated by the facts. Copies of reports in this investigation were previously submitted to the Department.   (97-25)

In 1948, information was received alleging that one Abraham Teitelbaum, an attorney of Chicago, Illinois, first purchased a home in Palm Springs, California, during October, 1946. He reportedly had a $400,000 yearly income from property in Chicago, and it was indicated he was a member of the law firm of Melnick and Melnick. It is reported that the Melnick brothers of Mrs. Teitelbaum, who also is an attorney. Information further indicates that Teitelbaum owned the Tyted Corporation in Chicago, a holding company for his real estate.

cc: Mr. A. Devitt Vanech
Deputy Attorney General

December 6, 1951

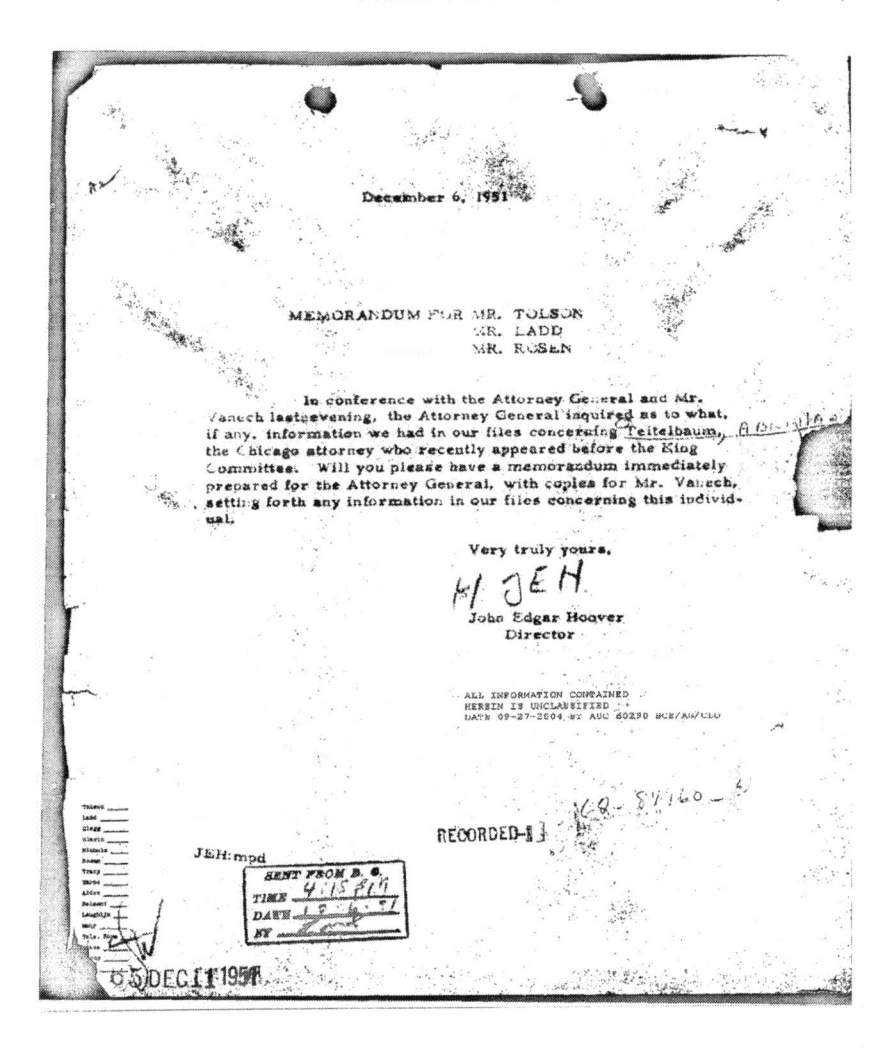

MEMORANDUM FOR MR. TOLSON
                MR. LADD
                MR. ROSEN

In conference with the Attorney General and Mr. Vanech last evening, the Attorney General inquired as to what, if any, information we had in our files concerning Teitelbaum, the Chicago attorney who recently appeared before the King Committee. Will you please have a memorandum immediately prepared for the Attorney General, with copies for Mr. Vanech, setting forth any information in our files concerning this individual.

Very truly yours,

JEH

John Edgar Hoover
Director

FREEDOM OF INFORMATION ACT (FOIA)

Tolson
Ladd
Nichols
Belmont
Clegg
Glavin
Harbo
Rosen
Tracy
Laughlin
Mohr
Tele. Rm.
Holloman
Gandy

b7C

CHICAGO--ABRAHAM TEITELBAUM, FORMER LAWYER FOR THE FAMILY OF AL "SCARFACE" CAPONE, HAS PAID THE GOVERNMENT $325,397 HE OWED IN BACK TAXES.
E. J. SAUBER, DIRECTOR OF THE INTERNAL REVENUE BUREAU HERE, DISCLOSED THE PAYMENT YESTERDAY AND MADE IT CLEAR THAT TEITELBAUM PAID THE FULL AMOUNT DUE AND THAT NO SETTLEMENT WAS MADE BY THE GOVERNMENT.
8/9--E1213P

ALL INFORMATION CONTAINED
HEREIN IS UNCLASSIFIED
DATE 09-27-2004 BY AUC 60290 BCE/AG/CLO

AUG 13 1952

WASHINGTON CITY NEWS SERVICE

FREEDOM OF INFORMATION ACT (FOIA)

Tolson
Ladd
Nichols
Belmont
Clegg
Glavin
Harbo
Rosen
Tracy
Laughlin
Mohr
Tele. Rm.
Holloman
Gandy

(TEITELBAUM)
CHICAGO--ABRAHAM TEITELBAUM, ONETIME CAPONE FAMILY ATTORNEY WHO IN 1951 TOLD A HOUSE SUBCOMMITTEE THAT WASHINGTON "INFLUENCE PEDDLERS" OFFERED TO SETTLE HIS TAX TROUBLES FOR $$500,000, WAS INDICTED BY A FEDERAL GRAND JURY TODAY ON TAX EVASION CHARGES.
INDICTED ALSO WAS HIS COMPANY, THE TYTED COMPANY. THE SIX-COUNT INDICTMENT SOUGHT $184,293.64 IN TAXES, INTEREST AND PENALTIES ON 1946-47 INCOME. IT CHARGED THAT MOST OF THE INCOME NOT REPORTED FOR TAX PURPOSES CAME FROM RENTALS ON WHICH THE INCOME REPORTS WERE SUPPRESSED, AND IN TWO COUNTS CHARGED HIM WITH PREPARING FRAUDULENT RETURNS ON THE INCOME OF HIS WIFE, ESTHER MELNICK TEITELBAUM, ALSO AN ATTORNEY.
TEITELBAUM, 47, ACKNOWLEDGED DURING THE TAX INQUIRY THAT HE WAS PAID $125,000 A YEAR BY THE CHICAGO RESTAURANT ASSOCIATION TO KEEP THE RESTAURANTS FROM HAVING UNION DIFFICULTIES.
1/22--N412P

ALL INFORMATION CONTAINED
HEREIN IS UNCLASSIFIED
DATE 09-27-2004 BY AUC 60290 BCE/AG/CLO

FEB 2 1953

WASHINGTON CITY NEWS SERVICE

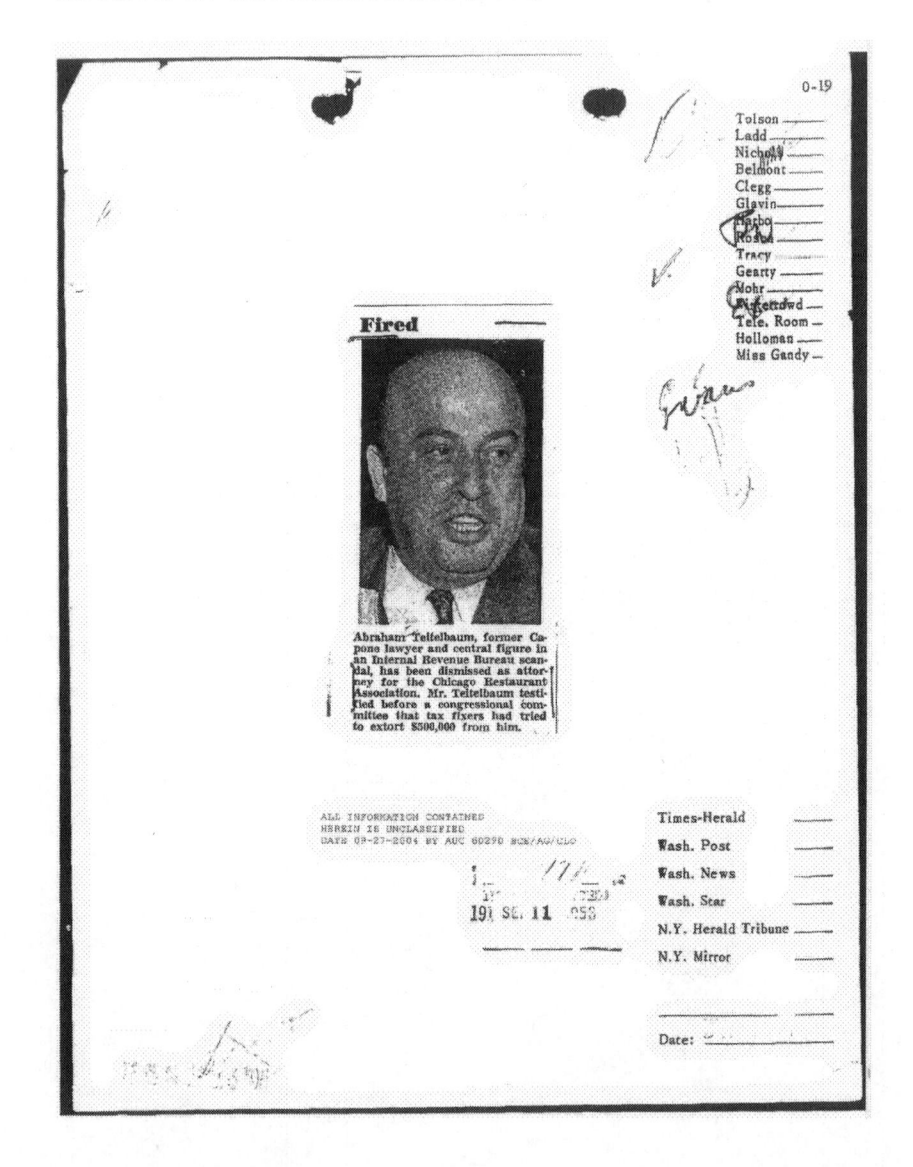

FREEDOM OF INFORMATION ACT (FOIA)

Fired

Abraham Teitelbaum, former Capone lawyer and central figure in an Internal Revenue Bureau scandal, has been dismissed as attorney for the Chicago Restaurant Association. Mr. Teitelbaum testified before a congressional committee that tax fixers had tried to extort $500,000 from him.

Ex-Capone Lawyer Indicted on Taxes

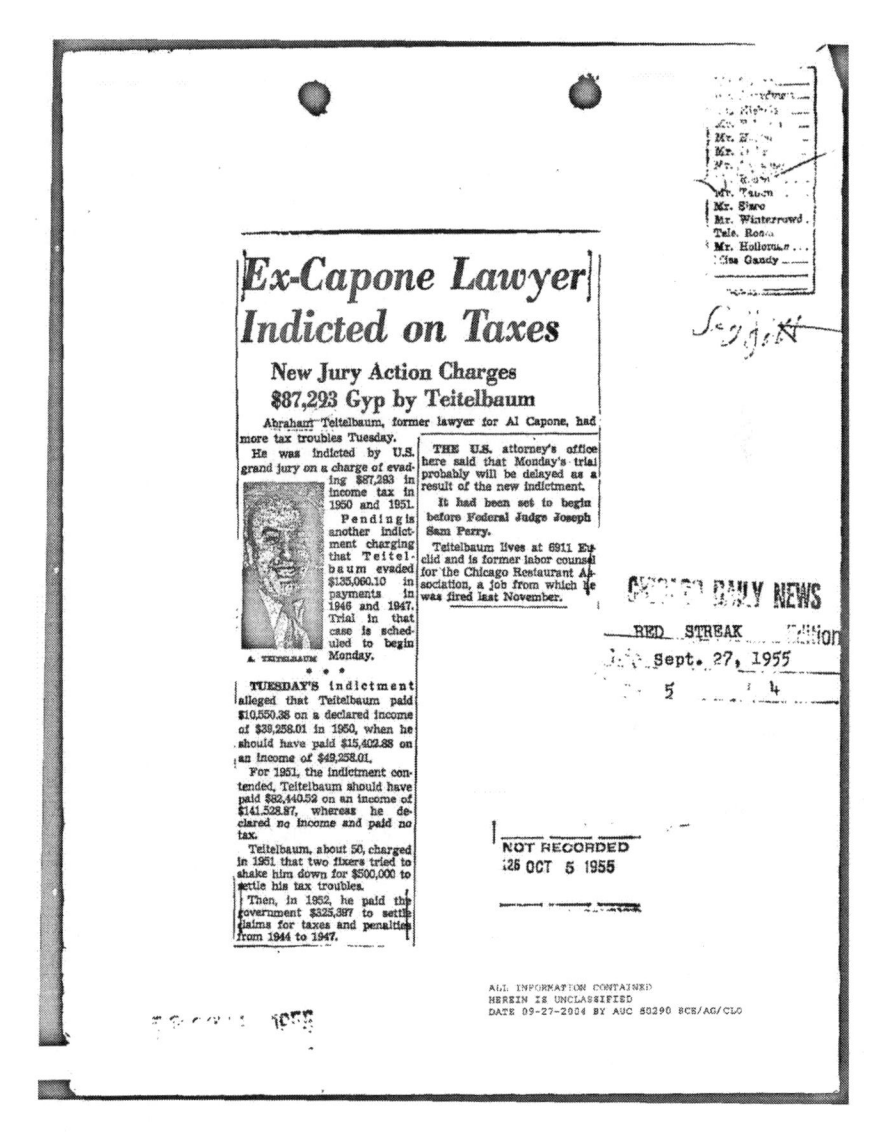

New Jury Action Charges $87,293 Gyp by Teitelbaum

Abraham Teitelbaum, former lawyer for Al Capone, had more tax troubles Tuesday.

He was indicted by U.S. grand jury on a charge of evading $87,293 in income tax in 1950 and 1951.

Pending is another indictment charging that Teitelbaum evaded $135,060.10 in payments in 1946 and 1947. Trial in that case is scheduled to begin Monday.

THE U.S. attorney's office here said that Monday's trial probably will be delayed as a result of the new indictment.

It had been set to begin before Federal Judge Joseph Sam Perry.

Teitelbaum lives at 6911 Euclid and is former labor counsel for the Chicago Restaurant Association, a job from which he was fired last November.

TUESDAY'S indictment alleged that Teitelbaum paid $10,550.38 on a declared income of $38,258.01 in 1950, when he should have paid $15,402.88 on an income of $49,258.01.

For 1951, the indictment contended, Teitelbaum should have paid $82,440.52 on an income of $141,523.87, whereas he declared no income and paid no tax.

Teitelbaum, about 50, charged in 1951 that two fixers tried to shake him down for $500,000 to settle his tax troubles.

Then, in 1952, he paid the government $325,387 to settle claims for taxes and penalties from 1944 to 1947.

CHICAGO DAILY NEWS
RED STREAK Edition
Sept. 27, 1955

FREEDOM OF INFORMATION ACT (FOIA)

Court Suspends Capone Lawyer

SPRINGFIELD, Ill., May 21 (AP)—Abraham Teitelbaum, a Chicago attorney who once represented Al Capone, today was suspended from practicing law for three years because he was convicted for income tax evasion.

The Illinois Supreme Court ordered the suspension rather than disbarment sought by the Chicago Bar Association because the Federal court in which Teitelbaum was convicted had refused to disbar or otherwise discipline him.

ALL INFORMATION CONTAINED
HEREIN IS UNCLASSIFIED
DATE 09-27-2004 BY ADC 60290 BCE/AG/CLO

Tolson
Boardman
Belmont
Mohr
Nease
Parsons
Rosen
Tamm
Trotter
Clayton
Tele. Room
Holloman
Gandy

Wash. Post and Times Herald
Wash. News
Wash. Star
N. Y. Herald Tribune
N. Y. Journal-American
N. Y. Mirror
N. Y. Daily News
N. Y. Times
Daily Worker
The Worker
New Leader

Date

0-16 (Rev. 10-28-57)

Tolson
Boardman
Belmont
Mohr
Nease
Parsons
Rosen
Tamm
Trotter
Clayton
Tele. Room
Holloman
Gandy

b7C

Court Won't Disbar Ex-Capone Lawyer

CHICAGO, Mar. 6 (AP).—The United States Circuit Court of Appeals ruled yesterday that Al Capone's former lawyer could not be barred from practicing in Federal courts because of two convictions for income tax evasion.

The lawyer is Abraham Teitelbaum, who for a time represented the prohibition era gang leader and the Capone family.

In an opinion written by Chief Judge F. Ryan Duffy, the Court of Appeals critized Robert Tieken, United States district attorney in Chicago, for appealing the decision of District Judge Philip L. Sullivan that the tax convictions were not grounds for disbarring Mr. Teitelbaum.

MAR 8 1958

ALL INFORMATION CONTAINED
HEREIN IS UNCLASSIFIED
DATE 09-27-2004 BY AUC 60290 BCS/AG/CLO

Wash. Post and
Times Herald
Wash. News
Wash. Star
N. Y. Herald
Tribune
N. Y. Journal-
American
N. Y. Mirror
N. Y. Daily News
N. Y. Times
Daily Worker
The Worker
New Leader

Date

FREEDOM OF INFORMATION ACT (FOIA)

0-19 (11-22-55)

Tolson
Nichols
Boardman
Belmont
Mason
Mohr
Parsons
Rosen
Tamm
Nease
Winterrowd
Tele. Room
Holloman
Gandy

Capone Family Lawyer Turns Up Broke

CHICAGO, April 25 (AP) — Abraham Teitelbaum, 50, one-time lawyer for gangster Al Capone's family, told a Federal judge yesterday that he is broke.

Mr. Teitelbaum said he is forced to act as his own attorney in the income tax evasion case against him and "after 27 years as a lawyer I have had to give up my practice and put my office furniture in storage."

ALL INFORMATION CONTAINED
HEREIN IS UNCLASSIFIED
DATE 09-27-2004 BY AUC 60290 BCE/AG/CLU

Wash. Post and
  Times Herald
Wash. News
Wash. Star
N. Y. Herald
  Tribune
N. Y. Mirror
N. Y. Daily News
Daily Worker
The Worker
New Leader

Date 4/25/56

0-19 (11-22-55)

b7C

Tolson
Boardman
Belmont
Mason
Mohr
Parsons
Rosen
Tamm
Nease
Winterrowd
Tele. Room
Holloman

Teitlebaum Guilty In Tax Evasion

CHICAGO, Jan. 25 (P).—A United States District Court Jury today convicted Attorney Abraham Teitelbaum, who once represented the family of gangster Al Capone, of evading $135,080 in income taxes.

Teitlebaum was accused of evading the income tax payment for 1946 and 1947 on undeclared income of $312,036.

Teitelbaum's counsel, George F. Callaghan, in final arguments yesterday, declared that "Shylock was a piker compared to the Government."

The attorney requested a new trial. Judge Joseph Sam Perry set February 10 for arguments and Teitelbaum was released on $2,500 bond.

ALL INFORMATION CONTAINED
HEREIN IS UNCLASSIFIED
DATE 09-27-2004 BY AUC 60290 BCE/AG/CLO

Wash. Post and Times Herald
Wash. News
Wash. Star
N. Y. Herald Tribune
N. Y. Mirror
N. Y. Daily News
Daily Worker
The Worker
New Leader

Date

0-19 (7-8-55)

Mr. Tolson
Mr. Boardman
Mr. Nichols
Mr. Belmont
Mr. Harbo
Mr. Mohr
Mr. Parsons
Mr. Rosen
Mr. Tamm
Mr. Sizoo
Mr. Winterrowd
Tele. Room
Mr. Holloman
Miss Gandy

b7C

Al Capone Lawyer Indicted Over Taxes

CHICAGO, Sept. 28 (AP).— Gang Czar Al Capone's lawyer was indicted yesterday for income tax evasion.

A Federal Grand Jury alleged the lawyer, Abraham Teitelbaum, evaded $87,293 in taxes during 1950 and 1951. Also pending against him is an indictment charging evasion of $135,060 in 1946 and 1947. The trial is scheduled for Monday.

ALL INFORMATION CONTAINED
HEREIN IS UNCLASSIFIED
DATE 09-27-2004 BY ABC 60290 BCE/AB/CLO

Wash. Post and Times Herald ___
Wash. News ___
Wash. Star ___
N. Y. Herald Tribune ___
N. Y. Mirror ___
Daily Worker ___
The Worker ___
New Leader ___

Date SEP 28 1955

FREEDOM OF INFORMATION ACT (FOIA)

Gets 12 Mos. Probation, Also Rebuked

BY ELGAR BROWN

Lawyer Abe Teitelbaum, convicted of $193,568 income tax evasions, escaped today with a sharp rebuke and 12 months' probation.

Federal Judge Perry, after a dissertation, imposed a 12 months' prison sentence but promptly suspended it "because you have had adversities."

Teitelbaum, 50, the bald and portly former counsel for the Capone family, appeared as affluent as ever but considerably chastened in spirit.

COSTLY SUIT

He wore a costly blue suit, white shirt, black tie and about 40 pounds of weight that he didn't used to have.

Usually voluble, Abe said nothing at all until after his "penalty" was announced, whereupon he thanked Judge Perry effusively.

His lawyers, George F. Callaghan and Melvin Klafter, also found it advisable to remain silent. The judge did all the talking.

STUDIES CONVICTIONS

He reviewed the two convictions of Teitelbaum, found guilty by a jury of evading $106,275 taxes in 1946-47, then pleading guilty to evading $87,293 taxes in 1950-51.

Judge Perry said he had spent much time reviewing the case. He recalled Teitelbaum had finally paid $334,050.72 taxes, penalties and interest for 1946-47, but pointed out:

"This was not a voluntary act, it was made only after a jeopardy assessment had been leveled against you. Then, surprisingly, you appear to have started slinging your money around.

"I have checked for precedents, and I think the government would have been foolish had it not indicted you, in spite of your belated payments."

AMAZING RETURNS

As to the second case against Teitelbaum, the court said it found the lawyer had made "amazing returns" on his 1950-51 incomes. The judge commented:

"It looked to me like you were trying to recoup the taxes you had been forced to pay by filing returns in which you claimed expenditures you never made.

"It is true the power to collect taxes can be the power to destroy, as your lawyers have argued. I have found you are currently a man without means—but I disagree with the theory that the government brought this about."

'GONE BROKE'

Judge Perry, in a sympathetic turn, observed that Teitelbaum has "lost his standing as an attorney" and has "gone broke," adding that he wouldn't even mention possible restitution on the 1950-51 tax bills.

Then he granted outright probation on the first conviction. On the second, he imposed and suspended the prison term and decreed the 12 month period of probation.

CHICAGO AMERICAN
DIAMOND FINAL Edition
Date October 4, 1956
Page 1   Col. 8

0-19 (11-22-55)

Tolson	
Nichols	
Boardman	
Belmont	
Mason	
Mohr	
Parsons	
Rosen	
Tamm	
Nease	
Winterrowd	
Tele. Room	
Holloman	
Gandy	

Gets Probation In $200,000 Tax Case

CHICAGO, Oct. 4 — Abraham Teitelbaum, fifty, former attorney for the family of gangster Al Capone, was put on twelve months' probation today for evading almost $200,000 in income taxes.

"It would be unrealistic and ridiculous to fine this man," Federal Judge J. Sam Perry said in imposing the sentence. "He has no money."

Teitelbaum originally was convicted of evading $106,275 in income taxes for 1946 and 1947, and later for cheating the government of $87,283 due in taxes on his income in 1950 and 1951.

Judge Perry said Teitelbaum apparently was trying to recover the penalties and assessments of $334,860 for the 1946-'47 offenses by cheating on his income in 1950-'51. He also noted that Teitelbaum still owes the government more than $100,000.

"I know you have suffered a great deal," Judge Perry said. "You have lost your business, had to close your law office. I believe the ends of justice can best be served by placing you on probation."

ALL INFORMATION CONTAINED
HEREIN IS UNCLASSIFIED
DATE 09-27-2004 BY AUC 60290 BCE/AG/CLO

Wash. Post and Times Herald	
Wash. News	
Wash. Star	
N. Y. Herald Tribune	
N. Y. Mirror	
N. Y. Daily News	
Daily Worker	
The Worker	
New Leader	

Date OCT 5 1956

0-19 (11-22-55)

Tolson
Nichols
Boardman
Belmont
Mason
Mohr
Parsons
Rosen
Tamm
Nease
Winterrowd
Tele. Room
Holloman

Capone Lawyer Put on Probation

Chicago, Oct. 4 (UP) — Abraham Teitelbaum, 50, former attorney for the family of gangster Al Capone, was put on 12 months probation today for evading $1,223,353 in income taxes. "It would be unrealistic and ridiculous to fine this man," Federal Judge J. Sam Perry said in imposing the sentence. "He has no money."

b7C

ALL INFORMATION CONTAINED
HEREIN IS UNCLASSIFIED
DATE 09-27-2004 BY AUC 60290 BCB/AG/CLO

Wash. Post and Times Herald
Wash. News
Wash. Star
N. Y. Herald Tribune
N. Y. Mirror
N. Y. Daily News
Daily Worker
The Worker
New Leader

Date OCT 5 1956

FREEDOM OF INFORMATION ACT (FOIA)

Chicago Daily Tribune
Thursday, May 22, 1958   F Part 2—Page 1

Suspend Atty. Teitelbaum from Practice for 3 Years

Abraham Teitelbaum, former attorney for the Capone family and former Chicago Restaurant association labor counsel, was suspended from practicing law for three years by the Illinois Supreme court yesterday because of his conviction for income tax evasion.

The court ordered suspension rather than disbarment, which had been sought by the Chicago Bar association, because the federal District court in which Teitelbaum was convicted refused to disbar or otherwise discipline him.

Faces Cafe Outlay Quiz

The moon faced, sad eyed, balding attorney whose affairs are scheduled for further inspection by the Senate rackets committee next month, could not be reached for comment.

The committee will question him about his payment of $49,800 to officials in four restaurant unions for "special promotional work."

Teitelbaum, once a wealthy man and a downtown property owner, was placed on a year's probation in October, 1956, by Judge Joseph Sam Perry on charges of trying to cheat the government of $135,000 in income taxes for the years 1946 and 1947. The judge suspended a one year sentence on a second indictment covering evasion of $87,000 for the years 1950 and 1951.

Robert Tieken, United States attorney, sought to have Teitelbaum barred from federal court on the basis of these convictions, but District Judge Philip L. Sullivan denied this. The United States Court of Appeals upheld Judge Sullivan's ruling that the sentencing judge did not regard Teitelbaum's convictions as "crimes of moral turpitude."

Suspension to Do It

However, yesterday's suspension will keep Teitelbaum from practicing in federal court because a prerequisite is membership in good standing and full certification by the Illinois Supreme court.

The Illinois Supreme court's decision was written by Justice Byron O. House of Nashville. It said that the evidence offered by Teitelbaum in opposing the Chicago Bar association's petition to disbar him "wholly fails to show an absence of fraud." However, the decision added that there were "extenuating circumstances."

CHICAGO TRIBUNE
Sports Final Edition
Date MAY 22 1958
Page
Part II

ALL INFORMATION CONTAINED
HEREIN IS UNCLASSIFIED
DATE 09-27-2004 BY AUC 60290 BCE/AG/CLO

5 7 JUN 5 1958

44 JUN 4 1958

Office Memorandum · UNITED STATES GOVERNMENT

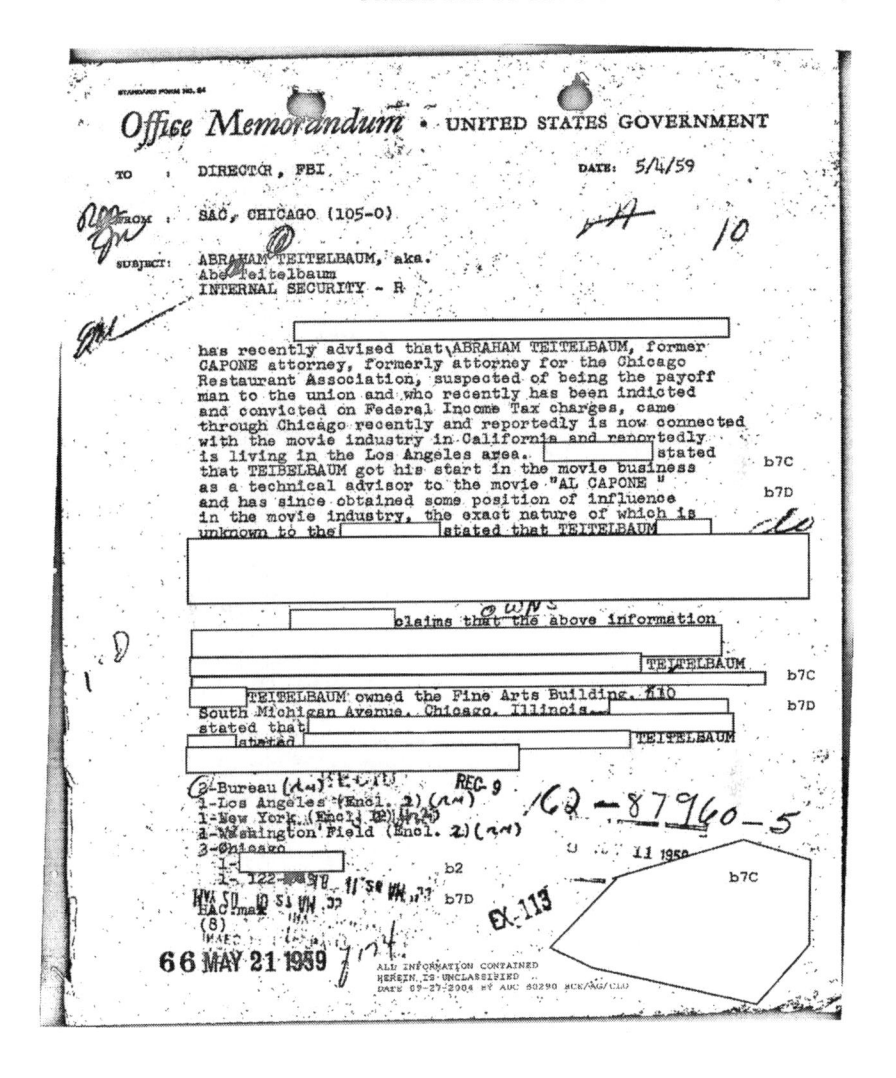

TO: DIRECTOR, FBI
DATE: 5/4/59
FROM: SAC, CHICAGO (105-0)
SUBJECT: ABRAHAM TEITELBAUM, aka.
Abe Teitelbaum
INTERNAL SECURITY - R

[REDACTED] has recently advised that ABRAHAM TEITELBAUM, former CAPONE attorney, formerly attorney for the Chicago Restaurant Association, suspected of being the payoff man to the union and who recently has been indicted and convicted on Federal Income Tax charges, came through Chicago recently and reportedly is now connected with the movie industry in California and reportedly is living in the Los Angeles area. [REDACTED] stated that TEITELBAUM got his start in the movie business as a technical advisor to the movie "AL CAPONE" and has since obtained some position of influence in the movie industry, the exact nature of which is unknown to the [REDACTED] stated that TEITELBAUM

[REDACTED] claims that the above information [REDACTED] TEITELBAUM

[REDACTED] TEITELBAUM owned the Fine Arts Building, 410 South Michigan Avenue, Chicago, Illinois. [REDACTED] stated that [REDACTED] stated [REDACTED] TEITELBAUM

From: The Hall Syndicate, Inc.
342 Madison Avenue, New York 17, New York
FOR RELEASE ON RECEIPT

9/21/59

INSIDE LABOR
By Victor Riesel

San Francisco — With the heat off, whimsy has overwhelmed the old Capone crowd. One of scarface Al's old comrades in arms — any calibre — now is opening shop in California and is advertising in the press for clients. His specialty in the protection business has been pushing hotel and restaurant unions around. Chicago got too hot after the McClellan rackets committee ripped the innkeeping and eatery business wide open.

So now that Bob Kennedy is an author and not an investigator, the old Capone arm, by the name of Abe Teitelbaum, has shifted to California. With Los Angeles as a base, he is holding open house for "friends and clients." At 9033 Wilshire Blvd. No less. Teitelbaum was the $125,000-a-year labor relations adviser to Chicago's restauranteurs for a long while.

Now he is telling the public brazenly that he has moved to Beverly Hills and that he has "represented for 15 years the Chicago Restaurant Assn. as labor relations counsel, also represented Greater Chicago Hotel Assn., Edgewater Beach Hotel, Arrington Hotel, John R. Thompson Restaurants, Toffenetti Triangle Restaurants, Alorzi Furniture Co., Chicago Candy Assn., Steinway Drug Stores and numerous others ...Friends and clients are "cordially invited to attend open house, formal opening on Monday, the 21st day of September, from two P.M. to five P.M."

There was nothing whimsical, however, about the reaction of some of the labor leaders at the national AFL-CIO convention here to the disdainful public soliciting of business by an old Capone man. They're disturbed. But, strangely enough, there has been no discussion of the mob at this parley — a discussion which dominated the last convention when the Teamsters were booted out into the icy Atlantic City sleet.

—MORE—

Victor Riesel   Page 2   9/21/59

Behind this silence on the mob, which still controls sections of powerful unions in Chicago, New York, several Jersey cities, some Pennsylvania areas and stretches of the midwest, is confusion over the real effect of the new Labor-Management Reporting and Disclosure Act. And despite all the noise you hear over Chairman Khrushchev and the steel strike it's labor's reaction to the new law which is the basic story of this hard working convention.

Under the new law, the government can go into the private life and activities of any labor official clean or crooked. The government can ask any union man any question. If a union official refuses to answer and takes the Fifth Amendment, he is unable to continue to hold office under the AFL-CIO Code of Ethical Practices. This puts the union officials on the spot.

Thus it is that Walter Reuther has told his own people that he wants the ethical practices code revised to give all union men the right to take the Fifth Amendment to cover their private lives and still retain public office in the unions.

There are other powerful leaders who want to kill off labor's own Ethical Practices Committee completely.

Some of the committee members, queried by this column, believe that the Ethical Practices Committee now could inadvertently prepare evidence which would send labor leaders to jail, instead of just disciplining them and directing them to clean up a union.

This, they believe, could happen if Section 601 of the new labor law is enforced. This section gives the Secretary of Labor terrific power to subpena all records, minutes, even notes taken at Ethical Practices Committee sessions. Under the still unexplored law, the Secretary of Labor has the power to order members of labor's own policing force even to report their private conversations to him.

The Justice Dept. could use the notes or minutes or private talks as evidence of wrongdoing in a union. The Labor Secretary and the Attorney General could then go into court seeking heavy fines and jail sentences for offending officials.

MORE

Victor Riesel   Page 3   9/21/59

Under these circumstances, some of the Ethical Practices Committeemen are saying angrily, "Let the government now police the unions. We just won't meet." They point out, for example, that, under the law, AFL-CIO President George Meany could be subpenaed. At present he receives special reports from his observers who keep their eyes on the Operating Engineers, the old AFL Textile Workers, the Jewelry Workers and the Distillery Workers. Soon there will be an observer inside the eastern Longshoremen.

These are confidential reports. Some -- such as those covering the old Johnny Dio union, the Allied Industrial Workers -- say that the union now is clean and the racket forces are out. Others, such as those covering the Operating Engineers and the International Longshoremen's Assn., report progress, but state that there are still some corruption pockets. The labor people believe they can clean these up. But they say that the private reports could be the evidence for a swift move by the Justice Dept. which could stymie the work of the Ethical Practices Committee.

So the labor people are quietly awaiting clarification of the new law. There is no McClellan racket busting committee. The new law won't be functioning for a while. So the heat's off and the boys are back. Small wonder they're whimsical,

(Distributed 1959 by The Hall Syndicate, Inc.)
(All Rights Reserved)

FREEDOM OF INFORMATION ACT (FOIA)

~~SECRET~~

Office Memorandum · UNITED STATES GOVERNMENT

TO : DIRECTOR, FBI   DATE: 6/11/59

FROM : SAC, WFO (105-30627)

SUBJECT: ABRAHAM TEITELBAUM, aka.
IS - R   b7C

Re Chicago let 5/4/59 setting out that ▮▮▮▮▮   b7D
of that office, ▮▮▮▮▮ stated TEITELBAUM

[b1 redacted block]

A copy of this letter is being furnished to the
Los Angeles Office inasmuch as that office is presently
conducting investigation in this matter. RUC.   (S)

2-Bureau   b2
3-Chicago (105-) (RM)   b7D
 (1-122-203)
1-Los Angeles (Info) (RM)
1-WFO
HEF:dil
(7)

ALL INFORMATION CONTAINED
HEREIN IS UNCLASSIFIED EXCEPT
WHERE SHOWN OTHERWISE

DATE: 09-27-2004
CLASSIFIED BY 60257/NLS/AG/CLO/AAG
DECLASSIFY ON: 25X 3.3(6) 09-27-2029

~~SECRET~~

LA 105-6653

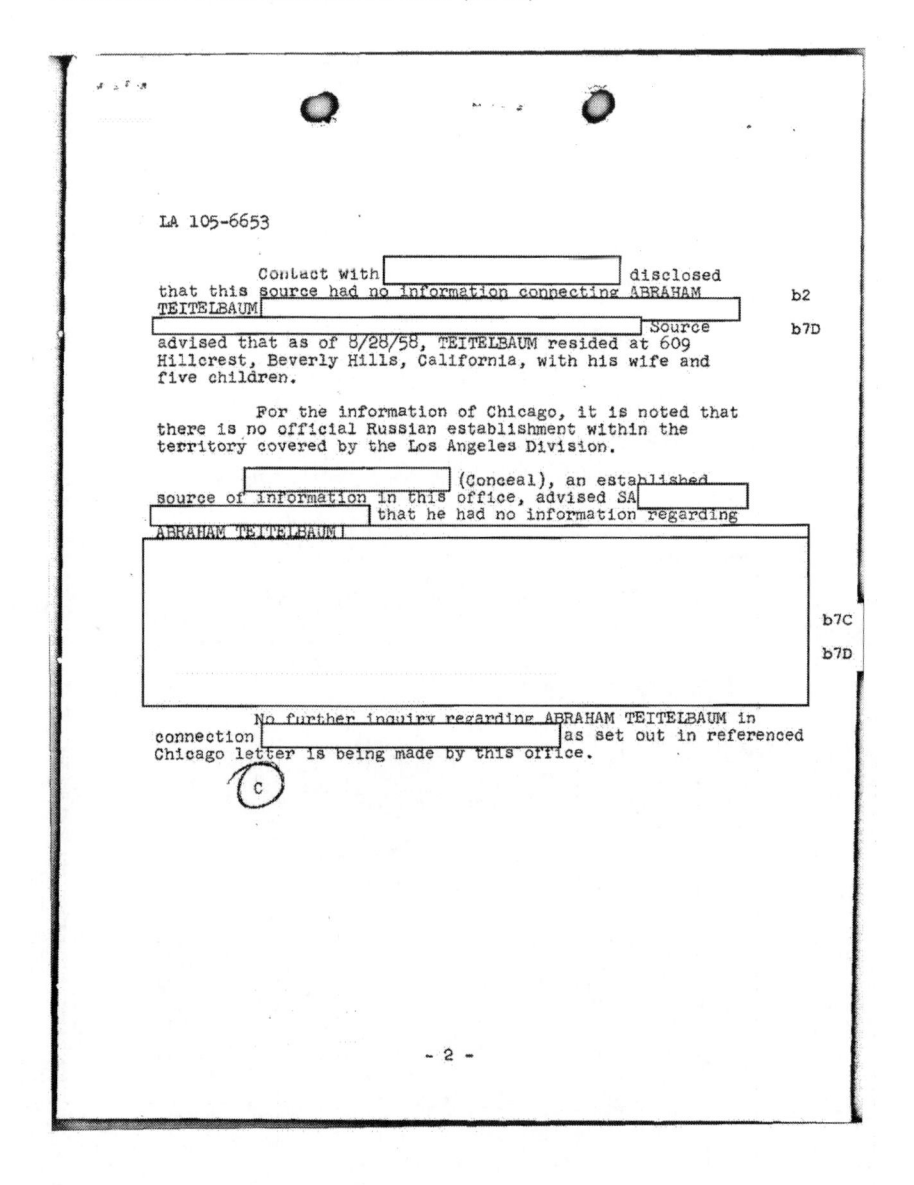

Contact with [redacted] disclosed that this source had no information connecting ABRAHAM TEITELBAUM [redacted] Source advised that as of 8/28/58, TEITELBAUM resided at 609 Hillcrest, Beverly Hills, California, with his wife and five children.

For the information of Chicago, it is noted that there is no official Russian establishment within the territory covered by the Los Angeles Division.

[redacted] (Conceal), an established source of information in this office, advised SA [redacted] that he had no information regarding ABRAHAM TEITELBAUM [redacted]

No further inquiry regarding ABRAHAM TEITELBAUM in connection [redacted] as set out in referenced Chicago letter is being made by this office.

C

CG 105-0

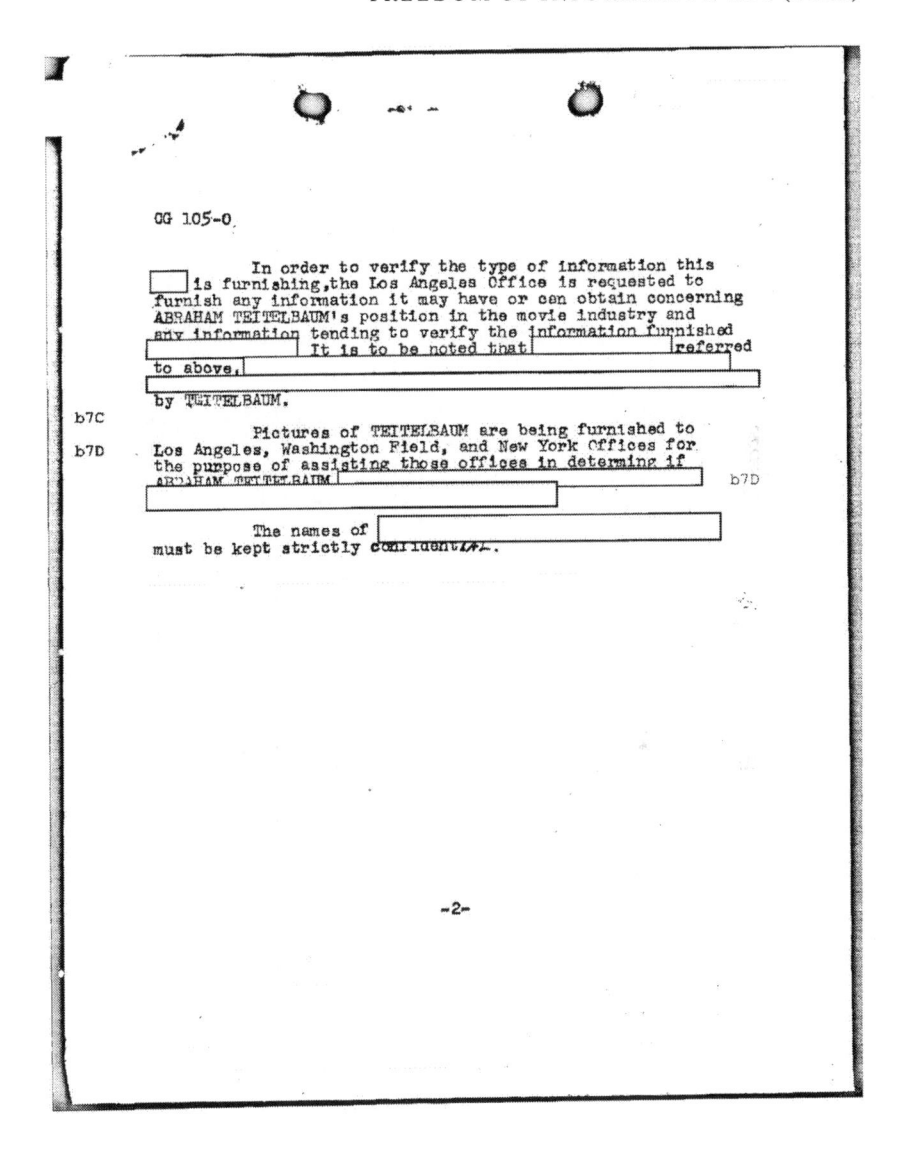

        In order to verify the type of information this [   ] is furnishing, the Los Angeles Office is requested to furnish any information it may have or can obtain concerning ABRAHAM TEITELBAUM's position in the movie industry and any information tending to verify the information furnished [   ] It is to be noted that [   ] referred to above, [   ]

b7C
b7D

by TEITELBAUM.

        Pictures of TEITELBAUM are being furnished to Los Angeles, Washington Field, and New York Offices for the purpose of assisting those offices in determing if ABRAHAM TEITELBAUM [   ] b7D

        The names of [   ] must be kept strictly confidential.

-2-

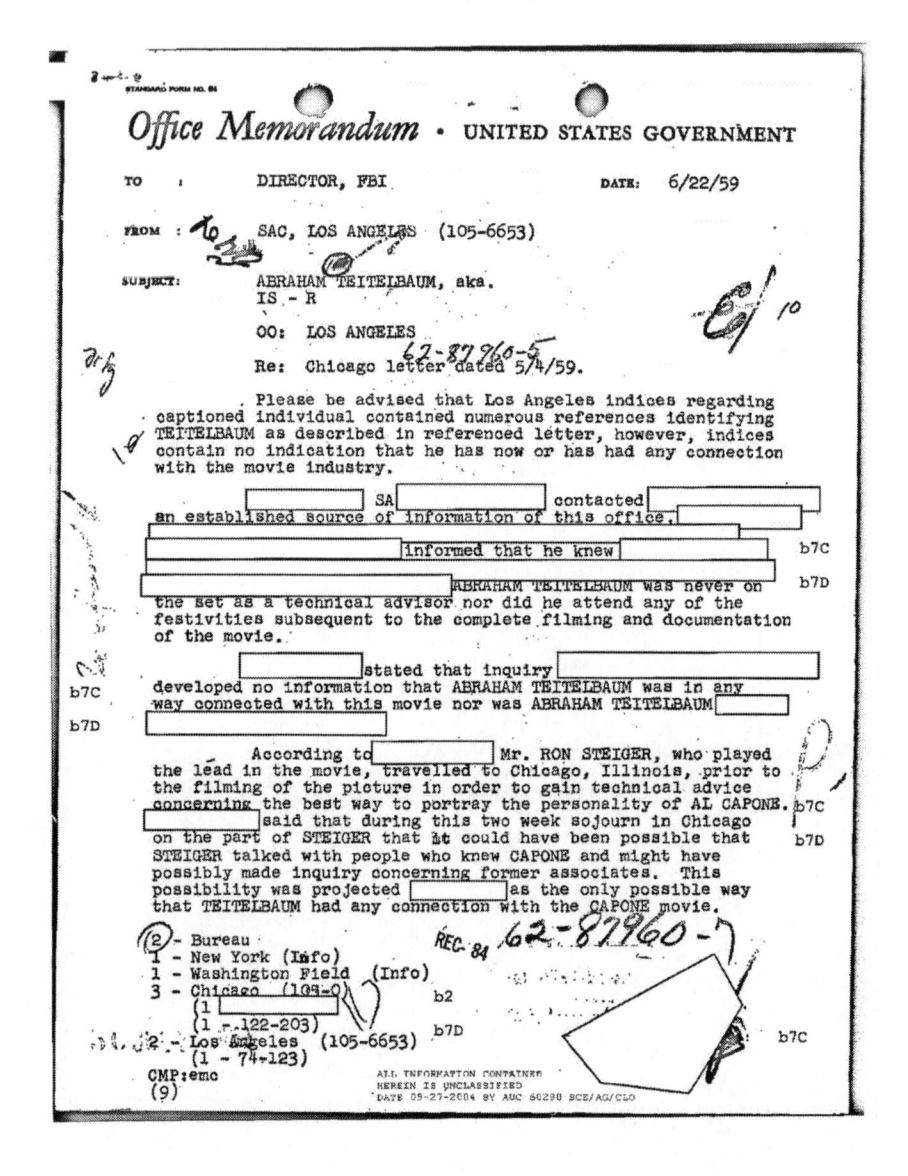

FREEDOM OF INFORMATION ACT (FOIA)

Office Memorandum • UNITED STATES GOVERNMENT

TO : DIRECTOR, FBI DATE: 6/22/59

FROM : SAC, LOS ANGELES (105-6653)

SUBJECT: ABRAHAM TEITELBAUM, aka.
IS - R

OO: LOS ANGELES

Re: Chicago letter dated 5/4/59.

Please be advised that Los Angeles indices regarding captioned individual contained numerous references identifying TEITELBAUM as described in referenced letter, however, indices contain no indication that he has now or has had any connection with the movie industry.

SA _____ contacted an established source of information of this office. _____ informed that he knew _____ ABRAHAM TEITELBAUM was never on the set as a technical advisor nor did he attend any of the festivities subsequent to the complete filming and documentation of the movie.

_____ stated that inquiry developed no information that ABRAHAM TEITELBAUM was in any way connected with this movie nor was ABRAHAM TEITELBAUM _____

According to _____ Mr. RON STEIGER, who played the lead in the movie, travelled to Chicago, Illinois, prior to the filming of the picture in order to gain technical advice concerning the best way to portray the personality of AL CAPONE. _____ said that during this two week sojourn in Chicago on the part of STEIGER that it could have been possible that STEIGER talked with people who knew CAPONE and might have possibly made inquiry concerning former associates. This possibility was projected _____ as the only possible way that TEITELBAUM had any connection with the CAPONE movie.

(2)- Bureau
1 - New York (Info)
1 - Washington Field (Info)
3 - Chicago (109-0)
  (1 _____)
  (1 - 122-203)
2 - Los Angeles (105-6653)
  (1 - 74-123)
CMP:emc
(9)

REC 84 62-87960-7

ALL INFORMATION CONTAINED
HEREIN IS UNCLASSIFIED
DATE 05-27-2004 BY AUC 60290 BCE/AG/CLO

SECRET

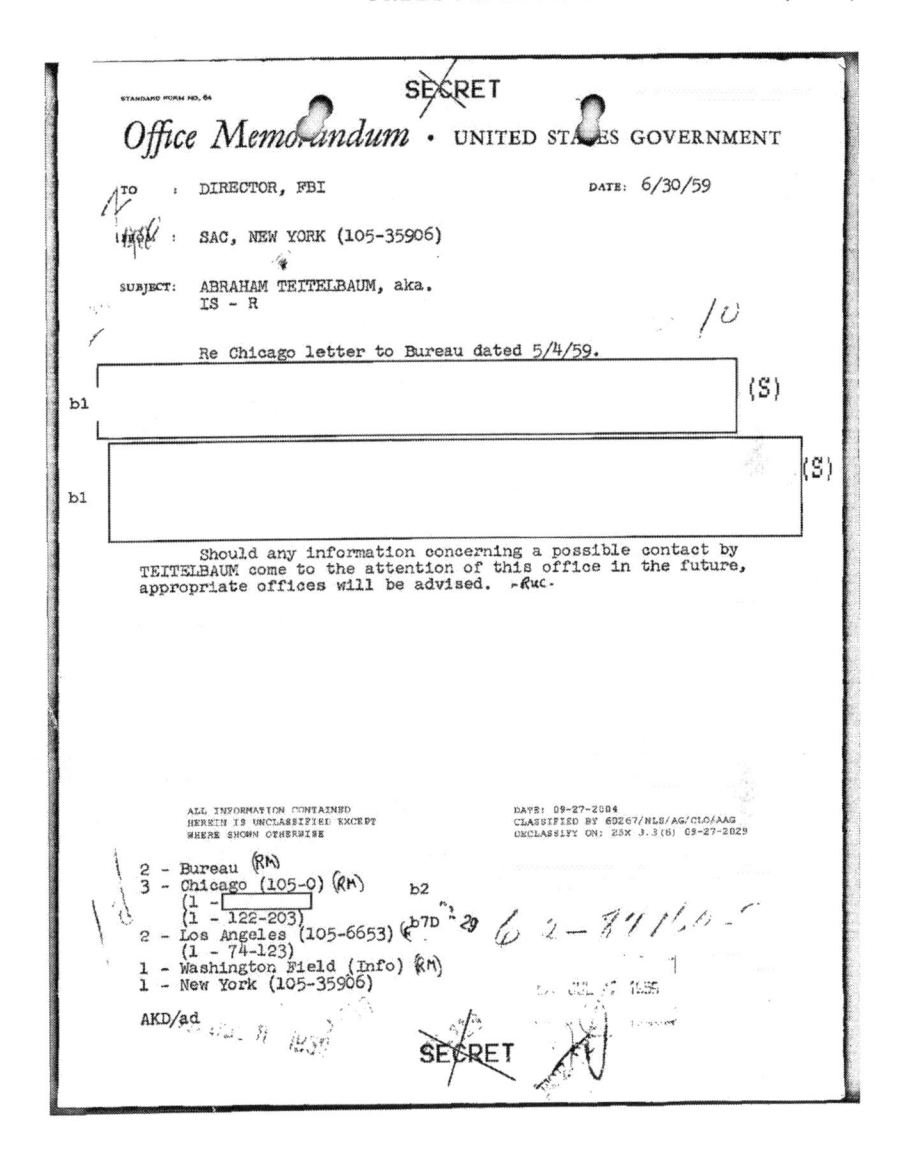

Office Memorandum · UNITED STATES GOVERNMENT

TO : DIRECTOR, FBI DATE: 6/30/59

FROM : SAC, NEW YORK (105-35906)

SUBJECT: ABRAHAM TEITELBAUM, aka.
IS - R

Re Chicago letter to Bureau dated 5/4/59.

b1 _____ (S)

b1 _____ (S)

Should any information concerning a possible contact by TEITELBAUM come to the attention of this office in the future, appropriate offices will be advised. -RUC-

ALL INFORMATION CONTAINED
HEREIN IS UNCLASSIFIED EXCEPT
WHERE SHOWN OTHERWISE

DATE: 09-27-2004
CLASSIFIED BY 60267/NLB/AG/CLO/AAG
DECLASSIFY ON: 25X 3.3(6) 09-27-2029

2 - Bureau (RM)
3 - Chicago (105-0) (RM)
  (1 - _____)
  (1 - 122-203)
2 - Los Angeles (105-6653)
  (1 - 74-123)
1 - Washington Field (Info) (RM)
1 - New York (105-35906)

AKD/ad

SECRET

FREEDOM OF INFORMATION ACT (FOIA)

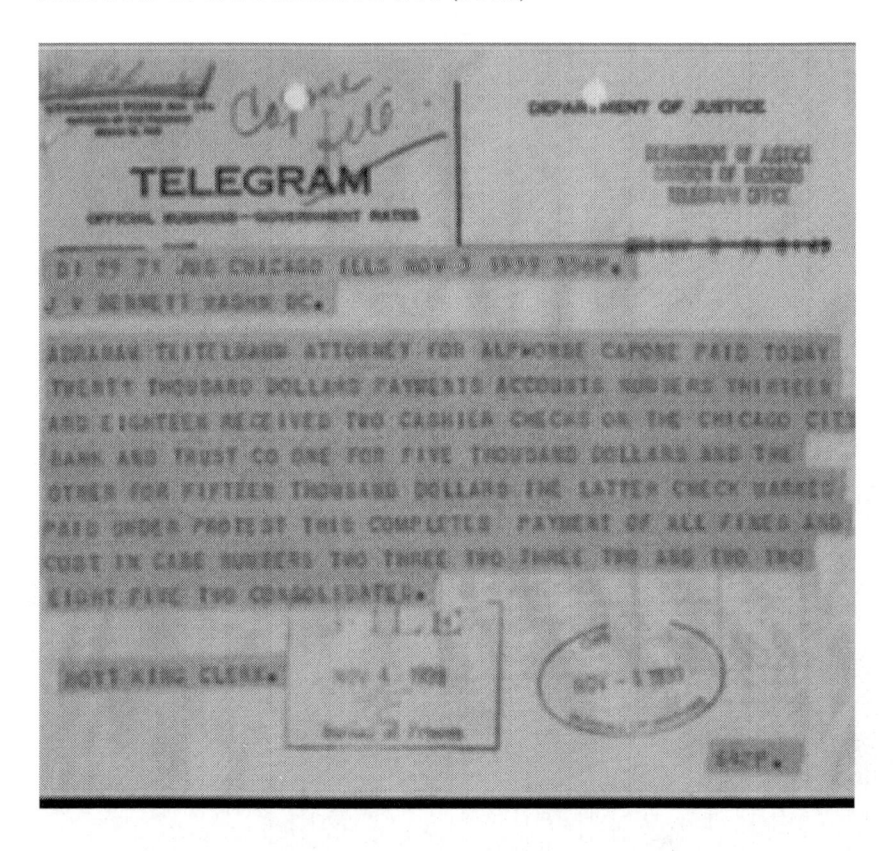

Telegram identifying receipt of payment of funds from Abraham Teitlebaum on behalf of Al Capone.

ALSO BY ROBERT J TEITELBAUM

Frogs Snails & Mobster Tales: Growing up in Al Capone's Shadow

For additional information visit our website at:

http://www.frogsandsnailsandmobstertales.com

Made in the USA
Columbia, SC
20 July 2019